Real Estate Matn Exam

A Precision Guide to Acing the Real Estate Test

Math Behind the Market

Math Tips and Tricks for the
Real Estate License Exam

Table of Contents

Introduction

Introducing the ultimate resource to help you understand the mathematical aspects of the real estate industry: the **Real Estate Math Exam** Guide. Regardless of your level of experience, aspirations, or interest in real estate, this book is designed to provide you with the mathematical skills and information required to successfully negotiate the intricate world of real estate transactions, appraisals, and investments.

Real estate investing involves more than just purchasing and selling properties; in order to make wise judgements, one must have a firm understanding of a number of mathematical principles. Math is essential to every stage of the real estate business, from knowing basic percentages and arithmetic to being proficient in more complicated formulas for financing, investment research, and property assessment. Taking this into consideration, we have crafted this book to act as a link, introducing you to the world of real estate via the prism of mathematics.

Our journey together will begin with the foundations of real estate math, where we'll brush up on basic math concepts that form the cornerstone of all calculations you'll encounter in the industry. We'll explore the **T-Bar Method, conversions between percentages and decimals,** and other essential tools that will prepare you for the more specialized topics ahead.

As we delve deeper, we'll tackle the art and science of **measuring and valuing property.** You'll learn how to accurately measure land and buildings, understand different property measurement systems, and navigate through the complexities of appraisals and value estimation. By mastering these skills, you'll be able to confidently assess the worth of real estate assets and make sound investment decisions.

Financing is another critical aspect of real estate that we'll cover extensively. From calculating **loan-to-value ratios** to understanding **mortgage payments** and **amortization schedules,** we'll break down the financial mechanisms that make **real estate transactions possible**. Our goal is to make you fluent in the language of real estate finance, enabling you to analyze loans, investments, and profitability with ease.

The book doesn't stop at **calculations**. We're also going to explore practical applications of real estate math in everyday transactions and strategic decision-making. You'll learn how to compute **commissions, determine buyer and seller proceeds, calculate property taxes,** and much more. These skills are indispensable for anyone looking to succeed in the real estate industry.

Investment and profitability analysis will also play a prominent role in our discussions. We'll guide you through evaluating investment opportunities, **analyzing profit and loss**, and understanding the nuances of **depreciation, capitalization rates, and the gross rent multiplier.** By the end of this book, you'll have the tools to assess the viability of real estate investments and strategize for maximum profitability.

Lastly, we'll venture into advanced concepts and practical tools that will set you apart as a real estate professional. We aim not only to educate but also to inspire you to become the go-to agent in your area, armed with knowledge and confidence.

To solidify your understanding and mastery of each chapter's content, you'll be challenged with **three exams designed to test your knowledge on the concepts covered.** These exams will help reinforce your learning and ensure you're well-prepared to apply these mathematical principles in real-world real estate scenarios.

This book is your companion on a journey to mastering real estate math. It's designed to be accessible, engaging, and, most importantly, practical. So, let's embark on this journey together, with a promise that by the end, numbers and calculations in real estate will not just be less intimidating but will become your trusted allies in making informed, intelligent decisions in the dynamic world of real estate.

Welcome aboard, and let's get started on this exciting adventure into the world of Real Estate Math Calculations!

Simple Real Estate Math

Basic Math Concepts

In the realm of real estate, a strong grasp of basic math concepts is indispensable. From calculating areas and understanding financial terms to estimating property values and commissions, math is the backbone of all real estate transactions. Let's delve into the fundamental mathematical concepts you'll encounter in the industry.

- *Arithmetic Operations:* Addition, subtraction, multiplication, and division are the basic operations you'll use daily. Whether you're calculating the total cost of a property, determining the difference in property sizes, or figuring out your commission, these operations are your basic tools.

- *Percentages:* A percentage represents a fraction of 100 and is a fundamental concept in calculating interest rates, commission rates, loan-to-value ratios, and more. Understanding how to convert percentages into decimals and vice versa is crucial for financial calculations in real estate.

- *Fractions and Decimals:* Real estate transactions often involve fractions and decimals, especially in measurements and financial ratios. Being comfortable with converting between the two and understanding their applications is essential.

- *Geometry:* Calculating the area of properties requires a basic understanding of geometry. You'll often use formulas for rectangles, triangles, and occasionally more complex shapes to determine the size of a lot or the square footage of a building.

The T-Bar Method

The T-Bar Method is a visual tool used in real estate to simplify complex calculations, particularly those involving prorations and allocations. It resembles a T-shaped chart where you balance two sides of a transaction.

For instance, when prorating property taxes, you list what is owed on one side and what has been paid on the other, balancing the equation to find out what the buyer or seller owes at closing.

Example: If property taxes for a year are $1,200 and the closing is exactly halfway through the year, the T-Bar Method helps you visually divide the responsibility between the buyer and seller.

Seller | Buyer
$600 | $600

This method simplifies understanding who owes what, ensuring fair and transparent transactions.

Conversions - Percentages and Decimals

Converting between percentages and decimals is a frequently used skill in real estate calculations. This conversion is straightforward but vital for accurately determining financial figures like interest rates, commission percentages, and more.

- **To convert a percentage to a decimal,** divide by 100.
For example, 25% becomes 0.25 (25 ÷ 100).

- **To convert a decimal to a percentage,** multiply by 100.
For example, 0.3 becomes 30% (0.3 × 100).

Application in Real Estate:

- *Calculating Commissions:* If a real estate agent earns a 5% commission on a $200,000 sale, convert the percentage to a decimal (0.05) and multiply by the sale price to find the commission amount: $200,000 × 0.05 = $10,000.

- *Determining Loan Interest:* For a loan with a 3.5% annual interest rate, converting the rate to a decimal (0.035) allows you to calculate the interest on the principal amount. If the principal is $150,000, the interest for one year would be $150,000 × 0.035 = $5,250.

Practical Exercises:

Commission Calculation: A property sells for $350,000 with an agent commission rate of 6%. Calculate the commission in dollars.

Interest Calculation: If you take out a mortgage of $250,000 at an annual interest rate of 4%, calculate the total interest paid in one year.

Area Calculation: A rectangular lot measures 150 feet by 90 feet. Calculate the area in square feet and convert it to acres (1 acre = 43,560 square feet).

Conclusion

This chapter laid the groundwork for understanding the essential math concepts in real estate. Mastery of basic arithmetic, the T-Bar Method, and conversions between percentages and decimals will serve as the foundation for more complex calculations and concepts discussed in later chapters. Engaging with these fundamentals through practical exercises will enhance your confidence and proficiency in real estate math, setting the stage for success in this dynamic field.

Practice Exam 1 : Simple Real Estate Math

Instructions:

Select the best answer for each of the following questions. Each question is based on the mathematical methods and basic math concepts covered in Chapter 1, including the T-bar method, conversions between percentages and decimals, and other foundational arithmetic operations.

1. What is 25% of $200,000?

A) $20,000

B) $50,000

C) $25,000

D) $5,000

2. Convert 0.75 to a percentage.

A) 7.5%

B) 75%

C) 0.075%

D) 750%

3. If a real estate agent's commission is 6%, what is their commission on a property that sells for $300,000?

A) $18,000

B) $1,800

C) $180,000

D) $18

4. A rectangular plot of land measures 100 feet by 50 feet. What is its area in square feet?

A) 5,000 sq ft

B) 150 sq ft

C) 15,000 sq ft

D) 500 sq ft

5. Convert 3.5% into a decimal.

A) 0.35

B) 3.5

C) 0.035

D) 35

6. If a property is listed at $450,000 and sells for $435,000, what is the percentage decrease in the sale price?

A) 3.33%

B) 5%

C) 3.5%

D) 15%

7. Using the T-Bar Method, if a seller owes $1,200 in property taxes up to the closing date, and the buyer is responsible for the taxes after closing, how much does each party owe if the closing is on June 30th? (Assume taxes are evenly distributed throughout the year)

A) Seller: $600, Buyer: $600
B) Seller: $1,200, Buyer: $0
C) Seller: $0, Buyer: $1,200
D) Seller: $700, Buyer: $500

8. What is the area of a property that is 150 feet long and 120 feet wide?

A) 18,000 sq ft
B) 27,000 sq ft
C) 17,000 sq ft
D) 15,000 sq ft

9. If an agent receives a commission of 5% on a sale of $500,000, how much is the commission?

A) $25,000
B) $50,000
C) $5,000
D) $250,000

10. Convert 50% into a decimal.

A) 5
B) 0.5
C) 50
D) 0.05

11. A home is purchased for $250,000 with a down payment of 20%. How much is the down payment?

A) $50,000

B) $20,000

C) $200,000

D) $5,000

12. If the annual property tax on a home is $4,800, what is the monthly tax amount?

A) $400

B) $200

C) $600

D) $800

13. A lot measures 200 feet by 150 feet. Convert the area to acres. (1 acre = 43,560 sq ft)

A) 0.69 acres

B) 1.5 acres

C) 3 acres

D) 0.5 acres

14. If a loan amount is $200,000 and the interest rate is 4%, what is the annual interest?

A) $8,000

B) $800

C) $80,000

D) $8

15. A property's listing price is reduced from $350,000 to $335,000. What is the percentage reduction?

A) 4.29%

B) 5%

C) 15%

D) 4.5%

16. How many square feet are in a property that measures 220 feet by 110 feet?

A) 24,200 sq ft

B) 2,420 sq ft

C) 24,000 sq ft

D) 2,200 sq ft

17. Convert 250% to a decimal.

A) 2.5

B) 25

C) 0.25

D) 250

18. If a buyer needs to borrow $150,000 to purchase a home and they have a 10% down payment, what is the price of the home?

A) $165,000

B) $150,000

C) $166,666.67

D) $135,000

19. A building is sold for $1,200,000 with a commission rate of 3%. How much does the agent earn in commission?

A) $36,000

B) $3,600

C) $360,000

D) $30,000

20. A square plot of land has a side length of 100 feet. What is its area?

A) 10,000 sq ft

B) 1,000 sq ft

C) 100 sq ft

D) 10 sq ft

Correct Answers for Practice Exam 1 : Simple Real Estate Math

1. B) $50,000

2. B) 75%

3. A) $18,000

4. A) 5,000 sq ft

5. C) 0.035

6. A) 3.33%

7. A) Seller: $600, Buyer: $600

8. A) 18,000 sq ft

9. A) $25,000

10. B) 0.5

11. A) $50,000

12. A) $400

13. A) 0.69 acres

14. A) $8,000

15. A) 4.29%

16. A) 24,200 sq ft

17. A) 2.5

18. C) $166,666.67

19. A) $36,000

20. A) 10,000 sq ft

Practice Exam 2 : Simple Real Estate Math

Instructions:

Choose the most appropriate answer for each question. The questions are based on the foundational math concepts, the T-Bar Method, and conversions between percentages and decimals covered in Chapter 1.

1. Convert 15% into a decimal.

A) 1.5

B) 0.15

C) 15

D) 0.015

2. If a property sold for $400,000 with a commission rate of 7%, how much total commission is paid?

A) $28,000

B) $2,800

C) $280,000

D) $7,000

3. A rectangular parcel of land is 250 feet by 340 feet. What is its total area in square feet?

A) 85,000 sq ft

B) 590 sq ft

C) 8,500 sq ft

D) 59,000 sq ft

4. Convert a decimal 0.2 to a percentage.

A) 20%

B) 2%

C) 200%

D) 0.02%

5. If an investor buys a property for $150,000 and sells it for $180,000, what is the percentage increase in value?

A) 20%

B) 16.67%

C) 15%

D) 30%

6. Using the T-Bar Method, divide $2,400 in property taxes evenly between a buyer and seller for a closing date of July 1st. How much does each owe?

A) Seller: $1,200, Buyer: $1,200

B) Seller: $2,400, Buyer: $0

C) Seller: $0, Buyer: $2,400

D) Seller: $1,400, Buyer: $1,000

7. What is 0.5% of $500,000?

A) $2,500

B) $25,000

C) $5,000

D) $250

8. A lot measures 120 feet by 80 feet. How many acres is this? (1 acre = 43,560 sq ft)

A) 0.22 acres

B) 2.2 acres

C) 0.5 acres

D) 1 acre

9. Calculate the commission on a $750,000 sale with a 5% commission rate.

A) $37,500

B) $75,000

C) $3,750

D) $375,000

10. Convert 40% to a decimal.

A) 4

B) 0.4

C) 40

D) 0.04

11. If $10,000 is put down on a $200,000 home, what percentage is the down payment?

A) 5%

B) 10%

C) 20%

D) 50%

12. Convert 0.055 into a percentage.

A) 5.5%

B) 55%

C) 0.55%

D) 550%

13. A square plot of land has sides measuring 150 feet. What is its area in square feet?

A) 22,500 sq ft

B) 15,000 sq ft

C) 2,250 sq ft

D) 225 sq ft

14. What is the annual interest on a $100,000 loan at a 6% interest rate?

A) $6,000

B) $600

C) $60,000

D) $6

15. A home's sale price is decreased from $500,000 to $475,000. What is the percentage decrease?

A) 5%

B) 25%

C) 2.5%

D) 10%

16. If a property measures 300 feet by 100 feet, how many acres is the property? (1 acre = 43,560 sq ft)

A) 0.68 acres

B) 6.8 acres

C) 1.5 acres

D) 0.5 acres

17. Convert 125% to a decimal.

A) 1.25

B) 12.5

C) 0.125

D) 125

18. A property is listed at $220,000 and sells for $210,000. What is the percentage decrease in the sale price?

A) 4.55%

B) 5%

C) 10%

D) 2.27%

19. If an agent earns a commission of 4% on a sale of $350,000, how much is the commission?

A) $14,000

B) $1,400

C) $140,000

D) $4,000

20. A plot of land is 90 feet by 110 feet. What is its area in square feet?

A) 9,900 sq ft

B) 990 sq ft

C) 10,000 sq ft

D) 1,000 sq ft

Correct Answers for Practice Exam 2 : Simple Real Estate Math

1. B) 0.15

2. A) $28,000

3. A) 85,000 sq ft

4. A) 20%

5. A) 20%

6. A) Seller: $1,200, Buyer: $1,200

7. A) $2,500

8. A) 0.22 acres

9. A) $37,500

10. B) 0.4

11. B) 10%

12. A) 5.5%

13. A) 22,500 sq ft

14. A) $6,000

15. A) 5%

16. A) 0.68 acres

17. A) 1.25

18. A) 4.55%

19. A) $14,000

20. A) 9,900 sq ft

Practice Exam 3 : Simple Real Estate Math

Instructions:

For each question, select the option that best answers it. These questions are derived from the concepts discussed in Chapter 1, focusing on basic math concepts, the T-Bar Method, and conversions between percentages and decimals.

1. Convert 20% into a decimal.

A) 2

B) 0.2

C) 20

D) 0.02

2. A real estate agent sells a house for $250,000 and earns a 3% commission. How much money does the agent earn from this sale?

A) $7,500

B) $750

C) $75,000

D) $7.50

3. Calculate the area of a property that is 200 feet long and 300 feet wide in square feet.

A) 60,000 sq ft

B) 6,000 sq ft

C) 600 sq ft

D) 60 sq ft

4. Convert 0.05 to a percentage.

A) 5%

B) 0.5%

C) 50%

D) 0.05%

5. If a property's selling price is increased from $100,000 to $120,000, what is the percentage increase?

A) 20%

B) 200%

C) 2%

D) 12%

6. Using the T-Bar Method, if $1,500 in property taxes is divided between the buyer and seller for a sale closing on May 31st, how much does each party owe assuming taxes are paid at the end of the year?

A) Seller: $625, Buyer: $875

B) Seller: $750, Buyer: $750

C) Seller: $1,500, Buyer: $0

D) Seller: $875, Buyer: $625

7. What is 2.5% of $400,000?

A) $10,000

B) $1,000

C) $100,000

D) $10

8. A lot is 90 feet by 120 feet. Convert this area to acres. (1 acre = 43,560 sq ft)

A) 0.25 acres

B) 2.5 acres

C) 0.5 acres

D) 1.5 acres

9. An agent receives a 6% commission on a $600,000 property sale. Calculate the commission.

A) $36,000

B) $60,000

C) $6,000

D) $360,000

10. Convert 60% to a decimal.

A) 6

B) 0.6

C) 60

D) 0.06

11. A buyer pays a 15% down payment on a $300,000 home. How much is the down payment?

A) $45,000

B) $15,000

C) $30,000

D) $4,500

12. Convert 0.09 into a percentage.

A) 9%

B) 0.9%

C) 90%

D) 0.09%

13. A square lot has sides of 100 feet. What is its area?

A) 10,000 sq ft

B) 1,000 sq ft

C) 100 sq ft

D) 10 sq ft

14. What is the annual interest on a $50,000 loan at a 5% interest rate?

A) $2,500

B) $250

C) $25,000

D) $2.50

15. The sale price of a home is reduced from $220,000 to $200,000. What is the percentage decrease?

A) 9.09%

B) 10%

C) 20%

D) 5%

16. If a property measures 400 feet by 150 feet, how many acres is the property? (1 acre = 43,560 sq ft)

A) 1.38 acres

B) 13.8 acres

C) 0.5 acres

D) 5.5 acres

17. Convert 175% to a decimal.

A) 1.75

B) 17.5

C) 0.175

D) 175

18. A property is listed at $300,000 and sells for $285,000. What is the percentage decrease in the sale price?

A) 5%

B) 15%

C) 10%

D) 50%

19. If an agent earns a commission of 2% on a sale of $450,000, how much is the commission?

A) $9,000

B) $900

C) $90,000

D) $9

20. A rectangular plot of land is 80 feet by 100 feet. What is its area in square feet?

A) 8,000 sq ft

B) 800 sq ft

C) 18,000 sq ft

D) 1,800 sq ft

Review your knowledge of Chapter 1 and apply the concepts you've learned to select the correct answers. Good luck!

Correct Answers for Practice Exam 3: Simple Real Estate Math

1. B) 0.2

2. A) $7,500

3. A) 60,000 sq ft

4. A) 5%

5. A) 20%

6. B) Seller: $750, Buyer: $750

7. A) $10,000

8. A) 0.25 acres

9. A) $36,000

10. B) 0.6

11. A) $45,000

12. A) 9%

13. A) 10,000 sq ft

14. A) $2,500

15. B) 10%

16. A) 1.38 acres

17. A) 1.75

18. A) 5%

19. A) $9,000

20. A) 8,000 sq ft

Understanding Property Measurements and Area

Understanding property measurements and area is crucial in the realm of real estate. It forms the basis for assessing property value, calculating taxes, and complying with zoning laws. This chapter delves into the methods and systems used to measure land and structures, offering insights into their historical backgrounds, practical applications, and mathematical foundations.

1. Area and Land Measurement

In real estate, understanding the area and dimensions of land is foundational. It influences property valuation, development potential, and regulatory compliance. The measurement of land area is traditionally expressed in square units (square feet, square meters, acres, hectares) and is derived from the shape and boundaries of the property.

Basic Concepts

- ***Definition of Area:*** At its core, the area represents the size of a two-dimensional surface. It is measured in square units, which could be square feet (sq ft) in the United States or square meters (sq m) in countries using the metric system. The choice of unit often depends on the standard measurement system used in the property's location.

- ***Calculating Area:*** The method for calculating the area depends on the shape of the land or property. Common formulas include:
  - ***Rectangle/Square:*** Length × Width. This formula is used for properties with straight, perpendicular boundaries.
  - ***Triangle:*** (Base × Height) / 2. Useful for properties or plots of land that include triangular sections.
  - ***Circle:*** $\pi \times \text{Radius}^2$. While less common in property measurements, it's useful for circular plots of land.
  - ***Irregular Shapes:*** Decomposing the shape into a combination of rectangles, triangles, and other shapes for which formulas are known, then summing their areas.

Practical Applications in Real Estate

- *Valuation:* The area of a property directly impacts its valuation. Larger properties often command higher prices, though value is also influenced by location, usability, and zoning restrictions.
- *Development and Planning:* Developers and architects use area measurements to plan buildings, parking spaces, green areas, and other features in new developments, ensuring efficient use of space and compliance with local regulations.
- *Agricultural and Rural Properties:* Area measurement is crucial for agricultural lands, where the price is often directly related to the size of the arable land.

Advanced Measurement Techniques

- *GIS and Satellite Imagery:* Geographic Information Systems (GIS) and satellite imagery offer advanced methods for measuring and mapping land. These technologies provide accurate area calculations, even for irregularly shaped parcels.
- *Surveying:* Professional land surveyors use a variety of tools, including theodolites, GPS units, and laser rangefinders, to measure the dimensions and boundaries of a property accurately. Surveying is essential for resolving disputes over property lines and ensuring accurate property descriptions in legal documents.

Challenges in Land Measurement

- *Irregular Shapes:* Properties with irregular shapes require more complex calculations and may involve dividing the area into manageable sections.
- *Topography:* Varied topography can complicate area measurements, especially in hilly or mountainous regions where three-dimensional considerations come into play.
- *Legal and Historical Boundaries:* Historical documents and legal descriptions may use outdated or imprecise methods for describing land boundaries, requiring careful interpretation and verification.

The measurement of land area is a critical skill in the real estate industry, providing the basis for valuation, taxation, development, and sales. Understanding the principles of area calculation and the tools available for measuring land can help real estate professionals, investors, and developers make informed decisions. Whether dealing with urban plots or vast rural lands, accurate area measurement is a cornerstone of successful real estate practice.

2. Measuring Structures (Homes and Buildings)

Measuring the structures of homes and buildings is a critical component of real estate valuation, listing, and marketing. Unlike land measurement, which deals with the area of a property, structure measurement focuses on the interior and exterior dimensions of buildings, affecting usable space, architectural design, and compliance with building codes.

Interior Measurements

Calculating Square Footage

The square footage of a building's interior is determined by measuring the length and width of each room and then multiplying these dimensions to get the area in square feet. These individual room areas are then summed to calculate the total interior square footage.

In real estate listings, certain areas, such as garages, unfinished basements, and attics, may not be included in the official square footage. Standards for what is considered "livable space" can vary by region and are often defined by local real estate associations.

Interior square footage directly influences a property's value and price. It is a critical metric for buyers and agents, serving as a basis for comparing properties and determining market value.

Practical Tips for Accurate Measurement

For accuracy and efficiency, use a laser measuring tool. It simplifies the process and reduces errors compared to traditional tape measures.

Always round your measurements to the nearest inch to ensure consistency and reliability in your calculations.

Keep detailed records of your measurements, including diagrams or sketches of each room, to support your calculations and provide transparency to buyers or appraisers.

Exterior Measurements

Measuring Building Exteriors

Exterior measurements of buildings often focus on the overall footprint, which includes the length and width of the building at its longest and widest points. For multi-story buildings, this may also involve calculating the height to understand the total volume or to estimate the exterior surface area for construction or renovation purposes.

Buildings with non-rectangular footprints require more complex measurement techniques, dividing the exterior into measurable segments.

Impact on Valuations and Property Listings

The exterior dimensions of a building can affect its valuation, particularly in commercial real estate, where the facade's appearance and the building's volume may impact its use and desirability. Accurate exterior measurements are essential for creating property listings that comply with legal standards and meet buyer expectations. Misrepresentations of building size can lead to disputes and financial adjustments.

Challenges in Structure Measurement

Gaining access to all parts of a building, especially in occupied or commercial properties, can be challenging but is necessary for accurate measurement.

Features like bay windows, recessed entrances, and architectural embellishments can complicate measurements.

Compliance with local building codes and standards affects how measurements are conducted and reported.

So, accurate measurement of homes and buildings is fundamental to real estate practice, affecting everything from property listings to valuations and legal documentation. By adhering to standard measurement practices and utilizing modern tools, real estate professionals can ensure that their property assessments are accurate and reliable. Understanding both the theory and practice of measuring structures is essential for success in the real estate industry.

3. Metes-and-Bounds

The metes-and-bounds system is one of the oldest methods of describing land, primarily used in the United States. This system relies on detailed descriptions of land boundaries based on physical features of the geography, distances, and directions. Understanding metes-and-bounds is essential for real estate professionals, especially when dealing with properties in regions where this system is prevalent.

Understanding the System

The metes-and-bounds system has its roots in England and was brought to America by early settlers. Its use predates the adoption of the more systematic grid-based land surveys.
Over centuries, the system has evolved, but its core principle of describing land using natural landmarks and precise measurements remains unchanged.

Description and Terminology

Metes: Refers to the measurement of distance and direction. Metes describe the bounds by stating the length of a boundary line and the direction it runs.
Bounds: Bounds describe the boundary lines of a parcel of land using physical landmarks (trees, rocks, rivers) or adjacent properties.
Terminology: Terms like "thence," "bearing," and "to a point" are commonly used in metes-and-bounds descriptions to navigate the reader through the property boundaries.

Practical Application

Creating a Metes-and-Bounds Description

Step 1: Establish a Starting Point: Identify a clear, permanent starting point (POB - Point of Beginning) for the description. This could be a natural landmark or a man-made marker.

Step 2: Measure and Record Distances and Directions: Using a compass and a tape measure or a surveyor's chain, record the direction and length of each boundary line, moving from the POB around the property until you return to the starting point.

Step 3: Note Physical Landmarks: Include natural landmarks or man-made features that coincide with boundary lines to provide additional clarity and verification.

Step 4: Legal Review: Have the description reviewed by a legal professional or a surveyor to ensure accuracy and compliance with local regulations.

Challenges and Solutions

Interpreting Descriptions: Older metes-and-bounds descriptions may refer to landmarks that no longer exist or have changed over time, making interpretation challenging.

  Solution: Use historical records and modern surveying technology (GPS, GIS) to reinterpret and verify the original descriptions.

Accuracy: Human error in measuring and recording distances and directions can lead to disputes.

  Solution: Employ professional surveyors to conduct or verify measurements, especially for high-value transactions.

4. The Rectangular Government Survey System (RGSS)

The Rectangular Government Survey System (RGSS), also known as the Public Land Survey System (PLSS), is a method used primarily in the United States to subdivide and describe land in a grid-like fashion. Developed in the late 18th century, this system was created to simplify the process of land division and to facilitate the sale and distribution of land in the expanding frontier.

Development and Purpose

The RGSS was established by the Land Ordinance of 1785 as a standardized method to survey and allocate land, primarily in the newly acquired territories west of the Appalachian Mountains. The main goal was to replace the often ambiguous and dispute-ridden metes-and-bounds system with a more organized and universally applicable approach.

Key Components

- *Principal Meridians and Baselines:* The RGSS is organized around principal meridians (north-south lines) and baselines (east-west lines). Each principal meridian and baseline serves as a reference for surveying and describing land within a specific area.

Townships: The system divides land into townships, each typically measuring 6 miles by 6 miles, and further subdivided into 36 sections of 1 square mile (640 acres) each.

Sections and Quarter Sections: Sections can be further divided into quarter sections (160 acres), quarter-quarter sections (40 acres), and so on, for more precise land descriptions.

Working with RGSS

Interpreting RGSS Descriptions

Understanding Legal Descriptions: A typical RGSS legal description might read, "NE ¼ of Section 14, Township 10 North, Range 8 West of the 6th Principal Meridian." This description provides a clear and standardized method to identify a specific parcel of land.

Decoding the Terms: Learning to interpret these descriptions is crucial for real estate professionals, as they specify the exact location and size of a property.

Calculating Area within RGSS

Basic Calculations: The area of a section (1 square mile or 640 acres) serves as the basic unit for calculation. By understanding the subdivision of sections, professionals can accurately calculate the size of parcels.

Practical Application: This knowledge is essential for a variety of real estate and land-use planning activities, including valuation, development, and conservation efforts.

5. Lot-and-Block

The lot-and-block survey system is a method used to simplify the description of land in urban, suburban, and developed areas. Unlike the RGSS, which is used primarily in undeveloped territories, the lot-and-block system is most commonly applied within platted subdivisions. It provides a straightforward way to identify individual parcels of land based on a recorded plat map.

System Overview

The lot-and-block system emerged as cities and towns grew and the need for a simpler method to identify parcels within developed areas became apparent. It is now widely used across the United States, particularly in areas where land has been divided into smaller, residential, or commercial plots. Central to the lot-and-block system are plat maps, which are detailed drawings that show the divisions of a piece of land into lots, blocks, streets, and public areas. These maps are filed with local government offices and serve as the official record for land descriptions.

Advantages Over Metes-and-Bounds

- **Simplicity and Clarity:** The lot-and-block system simplifies land transactions by providing clear, easy-to-follow descriptions based on established plots, as opposed to the more complex and sometimes ambiguous metes-and-bounds descriptions.
- **Efficiency in Transactions:** With parcels clearly defined and recorded, real estate transactions can be conducted more efficiently, reducing the need for lengthy legal descriptions and minimizing disputes over boundaries.

Utilizing Lot-and-Block

- **Interpreting Plat Maps:** Understanding how to read and interpret plat maps is essential for anyone working in real estate. This includes identifying the boundaries of lots and blocks, the layout of streets and alleys, and any easements or public areas designated on the map.
- **Legal Descriptions:** A typical lot-and-block description might read, "Lot 15, Block 3 of Oakwood Estates, according to the plat thereof recorded in Plat Book 12, Page 36, of the County Records." This description provides all the information needed to locate and identify the property within the subdivision.

Significance in Real Estate Transactions

- **Conveyancing:** The lot-and-block system streamlines the conveyancing process, making it easier to transfer title to properties by reference to the plat map and the lot and block numbers.
- **Zoning and Development:** Local governments use plat maps and the lot-and-block system to manage zoning laws, property development standards, and public utilities planning.

Challenges and Considerations

- **Changes Over Time:** Over time, subdivisions may undergo changes that affect the original plat map, such as redivision, annexation, or redevelopment. Keeping plat maps updated is crucial for maintaining accurate land records.
- **Discrepancies:** Discrepancies between the physical layout of a subdivision and its recorded plat can arise, necessitating adjustments or legal action to resolve ambiguities.

Practice Exam 1 : Understanding Property Measurements and Area

Instructions:

Select the best answer for each of the following questions based on the topics covered in "Understanding Property Measurements and Area," including Area and Land Measurement, Measuring Structures (Homes and Buildings), The Rectangular Government Survey System (RGSS), and Lot-and-Block.

1. What is the formula for calculating the area of a rectangle?

A) Length + Width

B) Length × Width

C) (Length + Width) × 2

D) Length / Width

2. How is the interior square footage of a building typically determined?

A) Adding up the exterior dimensions

B) Multiplying the perimeter by the height

C) Measuring the length and width of each room and adding the totals

D) Using the building's exterior dimensions and subtracting non-livable space

3. What is the primary unit of measurement in the RGSS?

A) Acre

B) Hectare

C) Section

D) Township

4. How many acres are there in a section under the RGSS?

A) 160 acres

B) 320 acres

C) 640 acres

D) 1280 acres

5. In a lot-and-block survey system, what document is essential for identifying individual parcels of land?

A) Deed of Sale

B) Title Report

C) Plat Map

D) Zoning Ordinance

6. Which term describes the boundary lines of a parcel of land using physical landmarks or adjacent properties in metes-and-bounds?

A) Metes

B) Bounds

C) Bearings

D) Coordinates

7. What is NOT typically included in the calculation of a home's square footage?

A) Kitchen

B) Attached garage

C) Bedrooms

D) Living room

8. How is a township subdivided in the RGSS?

A) Into 36 sections of 640 acres each

B) Into 30 sections of 1 acre each

C) Into 100 plots of 10 acres each

D) Into 25 parcels of 40 acres each

9. What does the term "plat" refer to in real estate?

A) A type of architectural drawing

B) A detailed map showing divisions of a piece of land

C) The foundation of a building

D) A legal document specifying property ownership

10. Which of the following is a characteristic feature of the lot-and-block survey system?

A) It uses natural landmarks for descriptions.

B) It is primarily used in undeveloped territories.

C) It identifies parcels based on a recorded plat map.

D) It is the oldest land survey system in use.

11. What is the significance of principal meridians and baselines in RGSS?

A) They are used to calculate the area of a plot.

B) They determine the height restrictions for buildings.

C) They serve as reference points for surveying land.

D) They indicate water rights.

12. In metes-and-bounds, what does "metes" specifically refer to?

A) The use of markers to denote property corners.

B) The measurement of distance and direction.

C) Descriptions based on topography.

D) Legal documentation of land ownership.

13. How many square feet are in an acre?

A) 43,560 sq ft

B) 10,000 sq ft

C) 5,280 sq ft

D) 1,742 sq ft

14. Which system is most likely to be used for describing property in a newly developed suburban area?

A) Metes-and-Bounds

B) RGSS

C) Lot-and-Block

D) Acreage

15. What purpose does a township serve in the RGSS?

A) It is a measure of distance.

B) It is a primary building unit.

C) It acts as a reference for land division.

D) It is used for agricultural assessments.

16. When reading a lot-and-block description, "Block 5, Lot 3" refers to:

A) The third section of the fifth township.

B) The third lot in the fifth block of a subdivision.

C) The fifth building on the third street.

D) The third floor of the fifth building in a complex.

17. The NE ¼ of a section in the RGSS equals how many acres?

A) 160 acres

B) 320 acres

C) 40 acres

D) 640 acres

18. Which tool is essential for a surveyor measuring land using the metes-and-bounds system?

A) A plat map

B) A compass

C) A zoning ordinance

D) An architectural model

19. In urban planning, the lot-and-block system is best suited for:

A) Describing farmland.

B) Allocating water rights.

C) Designing city streets and plots.

D) Surveying mountainous regions.

20. A "section" under the RGSS is best described as:

A) A square mile area.

B) A piece of land described using natural landmarks.

C) A block within a city.

D) A plot designated for commercial use.

Correct Answers for Practice Exam 1 : Understanding Property Measurements and Area

1. B) Length × Width

2. C) Measuring the length and width of each room and adding the totals

3. C) Section

4. C) 640 acres

5. C) Plat Map

6. B) Bounds

7. B) Attached garage

8. A) Into 36 sections of 640 acres each

9. B) A detailed map showing divisions of a piece of land

10. C) It identifies parcels based on a recorded plat map.

11. C) They serve as reference points for surveying land.

12. B) The measurement of distance and direction.

13. A) 43,560 sq ft

14. C) Lot-and-Block

15. C) It acts as a reference for land division.

16. B) The third lot in the fifth block of a subdivision.

17. A) 160 acres

18. B) A compass

19. C) Designing city streets and plots.

20. A) A square mile area.

Practice Exam 2 : Understanding Property Measurements and Area

Instructions:

Choose the most appropriate answer for each question. This exam focuses on the mathematical aspects of property measurements and area, including calculations for land and structures, as well as interpreting survey systems.

1. Calculate the area of a rectangular lot measuring 150 feet by 100 feet.

A) 15,000 sq ft

B) 1,500 sq ft

C) 25,000 sq ft

D) 2,500 sq ft

2. A triangular parcel of land has a base of 100 feet and a height of 80 feet. What is its area?

A) 4,000 sq ft

B) 8,000 sq ft

C) 40,000 sq ft

D) 800 sq ft

3. If a property described in the RGSS is ½ mile by ½ mile, how many acres does it contain?

A) 160 acres

B) 320 acres

C) 80 acres

D) 640 acres

4. A house's interior measures include two bedrooms (each 12x15 feet), a living room (15x20 feet), and a kitchen (10x10 feet). What is the total square footage of these rooms?

A) 630 sq ft
B) 560 sq ft
C) 690 sq ft
D) 500 sq ft

5. Convert an area of 1 acre to square feet.

A) 43,560 sq ft
B) 40,000 sq ft
C) 48,400 sq ft
D) 10,890 sq ft

6. How many sections are there in a township under the RGSS?

A) 36
B) 16
C) 32
D) 64

7. Calculate the area of a lot that is described as "the NE ¼ of the SE ¼ of Section 10." Assume one section is standard size.

A) 160 acres
B) 40 acres
C) 80 acres
D) 320 acres

8. If a building is 50 feet long, 40 feet wide, and has 3 floors, what is the total square footage of all floors combined?

A) 6,000 sq ft

B) 2,000 sq ft

C) 4,000 sq ft

D) 12,000 sq ft

9. A property is sold for $10,000 per acre. How much would a 5-acre parcel cost?

A) $50,000

B) $5,000

C) $20,000

D) $100,000

10. A rectangular field is twice as long as it is wide. If its area is 72,000 sq ft, what are its dimensions?

A) 400 ft by 200 ft

B) 300 ft by 150 ft

C) 200 ft by 100 ft

D) 600 ft by 300 ft

11. How many square feet are there in a parcel that measures 0.25 acres?

A) 10,890 sq ft

B) 43,560 sq ft

C) 21,780 sq ft

D) 11,325 sq ft

12. If a section in the RGSS is divided into four equal parts, how much land does each part contain?

A) 160 acres

B) 640 acres

C) 320 acres

D) 80 acres

13. A developer divides a 10-acre plot into equal lots of 0.25 acres each. How many lots are there?

A) 40 lots

B) 25 lots

C) 10 lots

D) 4 lots

14. The perimeter of a square lot is 400 feet. What is the area of the lot?

A) 10,000 sq ft

B) 1,000 sq ft

C) 5,000 sq ft

D) 2,500 sq ft

15. A property described by lot-and-block as "Lot 12, Block 9" within a subdivision sold for $200 per square foot. If the lot measures 50 feet by 100 feet, what is the total sale price?

A) $1,000,000

B) $500,000

C) $10,000

D) $100,000

16. What is the length of the diagonal for a square property with sides measuring 100 feet?

A) 141.42 feet

B) 200 feet

C) 100 feet

D) 50 feet

17. If a farm consists of two parcels, one measuring 120 acres and the other 80 acres, what is the total area in square feet?

A) 8,712,000 sq ft

B) 6,969,600 sq ft

C) 5,227,200 sq ft

D) 3,484,800 sq ft

18. A town's central park is shaped like a rectangle, 600 feet long and 400 feet wide. What is its area in acres?

A) 5.5 acres

B) 6 acres

C) 4.5 acres

D) 5 acres

19. How many lots, each measuring 0.5 acres, can fit into a 10-acre field?

A) 20 lots

B) 10 lots

C) 40 lots

D) 15 lots

20. An irregularly shaped property has four sides, measuring 100 ft, 150 ft, 100 ft, and 150 ft, respectively. What is the approximate area?

A) 15,000 sq ft

B) 7,500 sq ft

C) 10,000 sq ft

D) 12,500 sq ft

Correct Answers for Practice Exam 2 : Understanding Property Measurements and Area

1. A) 15,000 sq ft

2. B) 8,000 sq ft

3. A) 160 acres

4. A) 630 sq ft

5. A) 43,560 sq ft

6. A) 36

7. B) 40 acres

8. A) 6,000 sq ft

9. A) $50,000

10. C) 200 ft by 100 ft

11. A) 10,890 sq ft

12. A) 160 acres

13. A) 40 lots

14. A) 10,000 sq ft

15. A) $1,000,000

16. A) 141.42 feet (Using the Pythagorean theorem, the diagonal = $\sqrt{(100^2 + 100^2)}$)

17. B) 6,969,600 sq ft** (Total acres = 200; 200 acres * 43,560 sq ft per acre)

18. D) 5 acres (Area = 600 * 400 = 240,000 sq ft; 240,000 sq ft / 43,560 sq ft per acre)

19. A) 20 lots

20. A) 15,000 sq ft** (Since the property forms a rectangle, area = length * width)

Exam 3 : Understanding Property Measurements and Area

Instructions:

For each question, choose the best answer. This exam delves deeper into advanced mathematical concepts applied in property measurements and area, including interpreting complex survey systems and performing intricate area calculations.

1. A circular plot of land has a diameter of 100 feet. What is its area? (Use π ≈ 3.14)

A) 7,850 sq ft

B) 3,140 sq ft

C) 15,700 sq ft

D) 7,065 sq ft

2. An L-shaped property consists of two rectangles: one is 100 feet by 200 feet and the other is 50 feet by 100 feet. What is the total area?

A) 25,000 sq ft

B) 20,000 sq ft

C) 15,000 sq ft

D) 30,000 sq ft

3. If a quarter section is divided into four equal parcels, how many acres are in each parcel?

A) 40 acres

B) 160 acres

C) 80 acres

D) 10 acres

4. A property described as "the South half of the North half of Section 12" under RGSS measures how many acres?

A) 160 acres

B) 80 acres

C) 320 acres

D) 40 acres

5. Convert 3,000 square meters to square feet. (1 sq m ≈ 10.7639 sq ft)

A) 32,291.7 sq ft

B) 30,000 sq ft

C) 28,611.9 sq ft

D) 10,763.9 sq ft

6. A trapezoidal plot of land has bases of 150 feet and 100 feet, with a height of 80 feet. What is its area?

A) 10,000 sq ft

B) 20,000 sq ft

C) 12,000 sq ft

D) 8,000 sq ft

7. How many square feet are there in a township under the RGSS?

A) 93,240,000 sq ft

B) 23,040,000 sq ft

C) 101,376,000 sq ft

D) 36,000,000 sq ft

8. A hexagonal lot has sides all measuring 60 feet. What is its approximate area? (Use the formula: Area $\approx (3\sqrt{3}/2) \times$ side²)

A) 10,392.3 sq ft
B) 15,588.5 sq ft
C) 5,196.15 sq ft
D) 20,784.6 sq ft

9. The diagonal of a square property is 100 feet. What is the area of the property?

A) 5,000 sq ft
B) 10,000 sq ft
C) 7,500 sq ft
D) 2,500 sq ft

10. A property's eastern boundary is described as running "300 feet to a point, thence north 45 degrees east for 200 feet." How long is the eastern boundary in total?

A) 500 feet
B) 400 feet
C) 300 feet
D) 200 feet

11. If a lot within a plat is described as 0.15 acres, what is its size in square feet?

A) 6,534 sq ft
B) 3,484.8 sq ft
C) 6,969.6 sq ft
D) 4,356 sq ft

12. A farm is divided into three parcels of equal size. If the total area of the farm is 360 acres, how many acres is each parcel?

A) 120 acres
B) 90 acres
C) 180 acres
D) 60 acres

13. A rectangular swimming pool measures 25 meters by 10 meters. Convert the area to square feet.

A) 2,690.98 sq ft
B) 8,073.47 sq ft
C) 3,229.17 sq ft
D) 1,076.39 sq ft

14. A property shaped as an equilateral triangle has sides of 100 feet. What is its area? (Use the formula: Area = (sqrt(3)/4) × side²)

A) 4,330.1 sq ft
B) 8,660.3 sq ft
C) 2,165.1 sq ft
D) 5,000 sq ft

15. A landowner wants to fence the perimeter of a square lot that measures 0.5 acres. How long will the fence be?

A) 464.16 feet
B) 830.8 feet
C) 920.32 feet
D) 1,000 feet

16. How many lots, each 0.2 acres in size, can be created from a land parcel of 2 acres?

A) 10 lots

B) 5 lots

C) 20 lots

D) 8 lots

17. If the length of a parcel is triple its width and the area is 9,000 sq ft, what are the dimensions?

A) Length = 90 ft, Width = 30 ft

B) Length = 60 ft, Width = 20 ft

C) Length = 120 ft, Width = 40 ft

D) Length = 150 ft, Width = 50 ft

18. A developer buys a rectangular plot of land that is 4 times as long as it is wide. If the area is 88,000 sq ft, what is the width of the land?

A) 220 feet

B) 110 feet

C) 440 feet

D) 100 feet

19. If a rectangular yard is 150 feet long and has an area of 7,500 sq ft, what is its width?

A) 50 feet

B) 100 feet

C) 75 feet

D) 25 feet

20. What is the area of a property that is described by metes-and-bounds as starting at a point, running north for 100 feet, east for 100 feet, south for 100 feet, and then west back to the starting point?

A) 10,000 sq ft

B) 1,000 sq ft

C) 5,000 sq ft

D) 2,500 sq ft

Correct Answers for Practice Exam 3 : Understanding Property Measurements and Area

1. A) 7,850 sq ft

2. A) 25,000 sq ft

3. A) 40 acres

4. B) 80 acres

5. A) 32,291.7 sq ft

6. B) 20,000 sq ft

7. C) 101,376,000 sq ft

8. B) 15,588.5 sq ft

9. B) 10,000 sq ft

10. A) 500 feet

11. B) 6,534 sq ft

12. A) 120 acres

13. A) 2,690.98 sq ft

14. A) 4,330.1 sq ft

15. A) 464.16 feet

16. A) 10 lots

17. A) Length = 90 ft, Width = 30 ft

18. B) 110 feet

19. A) 50 feet

20. B) 1,000 sq ft

Valuing Real Estate

Valuing real estate is both an art and a science, involving various methods to determine the most accurate estimate of a property's worth. This chapter delves into the primary approaches used in real estate valuation, each offering unique insights based on different aspects of the property and market conditions. Understanding these methods is crucial for investors, appraisers, real estate professionals, and anyone involved in buying or selling property.

Appraisals and Estimating Value

Appraisals are fundamental to the real estate industry, serving as a critical tool for buyers, sellers, lenders, and investors to understand a property's market value. An appraisal provides an objective, impartial, and unbiased estimate of a property's value at a specific time, taking into account a wide range of factors including, but not limited to, physical characteristics, location, and current market trends.

Purpose and Importance of Appraisals

- *Lending Decisions:* Appraisals are crucial for lenders to determine the amount of money to lend to a buyer based on the property's value.
- *Pricing Strategies:* Sellers use appraisals to set competitive selling prices, while buyers use them to make informed offer amounts.
- *Tax Assessment and Appeals:* Property owners use appraisals to challenge high tax assessments.
- *Insurance:* Ensures property is adequately insured at its current value.

The Appraisal Process

1. Initiation: The process begins with the appraiser accepting the assignment, understanding the purpose of the appraisal, and gathering preliminary data about the property.

2. Property Inspection: The appraiser conducts a thorough inspection to assess the property's condition, size, features, and functional utility.

3. Data Collection and Market Analysis: Collect data on comparable sales, rental properties, and current market conditions. This includes analyzing neighborhood trends, zoning laws, and potential future developments that could affect the property's value.

4. Approach Selection: Decide on the most appropriate valuation methods (Sales Comparison, Cost, or Income Approach) based on the property type and the available data.

5. Reconciliation and Final Estimate: Analyze the data from the chosen valuation methods, reconcile differences, and arrive at a final estimated value.

Factors Influencing Property Value

- **Location:** Proximity to amenities, schools, economic centers, and the quality of the surrounding area.
- **Physical Characteristics:** Age, architecture, square footage, condition, and layout.
- **Market Conditions:** Supply and demand dynamics, interest rates, and economic indicators.
- **Use:** The property's current use, zoning restrictions, and potential for future use changes.

Challenges in Appraisals

- **Subjectivity:** While appraisals strive for objectivity, the interpretation of market data and property features can introduce subjectivity.
- **Market Volatility:** Rapid changes in the real estate market can affect the accuracy of an appraisal over time.
- **Data Availability:** The lack of recent comparable sales in certain areas can complicate the appraisal process.

Appraisals are a critical component of the real estate transaction process, providing essential information for decision-making. Understanding the appraisal process, the factors that influence property value, and the challenges involved allows stakeholders to navigate the complexities of real estate valuation with confidence. Through meticulous inspection, data analysis, and the application of relevant appraisal methodologies, appraisers deliver valuable insights into a property's worth.

Practice Exercise:

Conduct a mock appraisal of a residential property by outlining the steps you would take from initiation to presenting the final estimated value. Include considerations for location, physical characteristics, and market conditions that would influence your valuation.

To solve the practice exercise, let's conduct a mock appraisal of a hypothetical residential property. The property in question is a single-family home located in a suburban neighborhood.

Mock Appraisal of a Residential Property

Step 1: Initiation
- ***Purpose:*** To determine the market value of the property for a potential sale.
- ***Client:*** The homeowner.
- ***Property Information:*** A 2,000 square foot single-family home with 4 bedrooms and 3 bathrooms, built in 2005.

Step 2: Property Inspection
- ***Physical Inspection:*** Assess the condition of the property, noting any updates or repairs needed. The property has a well-maintained garden, a two-car garage, and recent kitchen and bathroom upgrades.
- ***Location:*** Situated in a desirable suburban neighborhood, close to good schools, parks, and shopping centers, enhancing its appeal.

Step 3: Data Collection and Market Analysis
- ***Comparable Sales (Comps):*** Identify 3 comparable properties that have sold in the last 6 months within a 1-mile radius. Adjustments will be made for differences in size, condition, and features.
- ***Market Trends:*** Analyze current market conditions, noting that the market is currently a seller's market with low inventory and high demand, potentially increasing the property's value.

Comparable Properties:

Comp 1: Sold for $350,000 - 1,900 sq ft, 4 bed/2 bath, similar location, no recent updates.

Comp 2: Sold for $375,000 - 2,100 sq ft, 4 bed/3 bath, with pool, similar location.

Comp 3: Sold for $340,000 - 2,000 sq ft, 4 bed/3 bath, similar location, but requires significant updates.

Step 4: Approach Selection

- *Sales Comparison Approach:* Given the availability of comparable sales data and the property's residential use, this approach is selected as the most appropriate for determining the property's market value.

Step 5: Reconciliation and Final Estimate

- **Adjustments:**

   - *Comp 1:* Adjust upward for lack of updates (+$10,000).

   - *Comp 2:* Adjust downward for the pool feature (-$25,000) as the subject property does not have a pool.

   - *Comp 3:* Adjust upward due to the condition and updates of the subject property (+$15,000).

- **Estimated Value:** Based on the adjustments and analysis, the estimated market value of the subject property is determined to be approximately $360,000.

Considerations:

- *Location:* The property's location in a desirable neighborhood supports a higher valuation due to proximity to amenities and schools.

- *Physical Characteristics:* The property's condition, recent updates, and size are in line with or exceed those of the comparable sales, justifying adjustments to their sale prices.

- *Market Conditions:* The current seller's market conditions, characterized by high demand and low inventory, are likely to favor a higher valuation, as indicated by the final estimated value.

At the end of the mock appraisal, the property in question is valued at $360,000. This estimated market value is shared with the homeowner, complete with a comprehensive report detailing the process followed, the similar sales examined, the adjustments applied, and the reasoning behind the final valuation. This open and clear method makes sure the homeowner grasps the market value of their home and what affects it.

This mock appraisal exercise offers a hands-on look at the methods and factors appraisers think about when determining the value of homes, giving a real-world example of how they figure out what a property is worth.

2. Sales / Market Comparison Approach

The Sales / Market Comparison Approach is a cornerstone in real estate valuation, especially for residential properties. It bases a property's value on the prices of similar properties (comparables or "comps") that have recently sold in the same market. This approach assumes that the market conditions reflected in recent sales provide the best indicator of a property's current value.

Principle of Substitution

- *Foundation:* The approach is grounded in the principle of substitution, which posits that a rational buyer would not pay more for a property than the cost of an equivalent substitute.
- *Implication:* This principle guides the selection of comparables and the adjustment process, ensuring that the comparisons are as direct and relevant as possible.

Selecting Comparables

- *Criteria for Selection:* Comparable properties should match the subject property as closely as possible in terms of location, size, condition, and amenities. Key factors include the property type, square footage, number of bedrooms and bathrooms, lot size, and unique features.
- *Adjustments:* No two properties are exactly alike, necessitating adjustments to the sale prices of comparables for differences that affect value. Adjustments may be made for age, condition, location nuances, size discrepancies, and the presence or absence of certain amenities.

Adjustment Process

1. Quantitative Adjustments: These are adjustments for which a market-derived dollar amount can be directly applied, such as differences in living area square footage.

2. Qualitative Adjustments: These adjustments are more subjective, accounting for factors like location desirability, architectural style, and the quality of finishes.

Application and Limitations

This approach is particularly effective in active markets with a high volume of transactions, providing a robust dataset for comparison.
Its reliability diminishes in markets with few sales or when the subject property is highly unique, making it challenging to find suitable comparables.

Steps in Applying the Sales / Market Comparison Approach

1. Data Collection: Gather data on recent sales of comparable properties within a defined proximity to the subject property.

2. Initial Comparability Assessment: Screen potential comparables based on basic criteria such as property type, use, and location.

3. Detailed Analysis: Examine the selected comparables in detail, considering all aspects that could influence value.

4. Adjustments and Valuation: Apply necessary adjustments to the sale prices of the comparables to account for differences, deriving an adjusted value range for the subject property.

5. Final Value Estimation: Use the adjusted values of the comparables to estimate the market value of the subject property, often arriving at a value within a range indicated by the comparables.

The Sales / Market Comparison Approach is a dynamic and nuanced method that relies on the appraiser's expertise to interpret market signals and adjust comparables appropriately. It's a reflection of the market's collective judgment on value, providing a transparent and understandable valuation basis. However, its accuracy is directly tied to the availability of relevant market data and the skill with which adjustments are made.

Practice Exercise:

Select a residential property in your area and conduct a mock valuation using the Sales / Market Comparison Approach. Identify at least three comparables, list the reasons for adjustments, and estimate the property's value based on your analysis.

To solve the practice exercise, let's conduct a mock valuation of a hypothetical residential property using the Sales / Market Comparison Approach. We'll choose a single-family home located in a suburban area as the subject property.

Subject Property Details:
- *Location:* Suburban neighborhood, Anytown, USA
- *Property Type:* Single-family home
- *Size:* 2,000 square feet
- *Bedrooms/Bathrooms:* 3 beds/2 baths
- *Special Features:* Recently renovated kitchen, two-car garage
- *Lot Size:* 0.25 acres

Step 1: Data Collection
Identify three recently sold properties in the same neighborhood with similar characteristics.

Comparable Properties:

Comp 1:
  - *Sale Price:* $300,000
  - *Size:* 1,900 square feet

- **Bedrooms/Bathrooms:** 3 beds/2 baths
- **Special Features:** Basic kitchen, two-car garage
- **Lot Size:** 0.20 acres
- **Sale Date:** 3 months ago

Comp 2:

- **Sale Price:** $320,000
- **Size:** 2,100 square feet
- **Bedrooms/Bathrooms:** 4 beds/3 baths
- **Special Features:** Modern kitchen, no garage
- **Lot Size:** 0.25 acres
- **Sale Date:** 2 months ago

Comp 3:

- **Sale Price:** $310,000
- **Size:** 2,000 square feet
- **Bedrooms/Bathrooms:** 3 beds/2 baths
- **Special Features:** Basic kitchen, one-car garage
- **Lot Size:** 0.25 acres
- **Sale Date:** 1 month ago

Step 2: Initial Comparability Assessment

All three comps are similar to the subject property in terms of size, location, and general characteristics, making them suitable for comparison.

Step 3: Detailed Analysis and Adjustment

Comp 1 Adjustments:

- **Size:** Add $5,000 for smaller size.
- **Kitchen:** Add $15,000 for the less modern kitchen.
- **Lot Size:** Add $5,000 for smaller lot.
- **Adjusted Price:** $325,000

Comp 2 Adjustments:

  - *Size:* Subtract $5,000 for larger size.

  - *Bedrooms/Bathrooms:* Subtract $10,000 for extra bed/bath.

  - *Garage:* Add $10,000 for lack of garage.

  - *Adjusted Price:* $315,000

Comp 3 Adjustments:

  - *Kitchen:* Add $15,000 for the less modern kitchen.

  - *Garage:* Add $5,000 for smaller garage.

  - *Adjusted Price:* $330,000

Step 4: Final Value Estimation

Based on the adjusted sale prices of the comparable properties, the estimated market value of the subject property is calculated by averaging the adjusted prices of the comps:

- *Average Adjusted Price:* ($325,000 + $315,000 + $330,000) / 3 = $323,333

Taking into account the property's size, condition, and the current market trends as shown by similar sales, the estimated market value of the property is around $323,000.

This practice exercise showcases the Sales/Market Comparison Approach in action, emphasizing the need to choose suitable comparable properties and make precise adjustments to account for differences between the property in question and the comparable sales.

Cost Approach

The Cost Approach to real estate valuation is based on the principle that a buyer should not pay more for a property than it would cost to build an equivalent. The approach calculates the value of a property as the sum of the land value plus the current cost of constructing improvements minus depreciation. This method is particularly useful for valuing special-purpose or unique properties, where comparable sales or income data may be limited.

Principle of the Cost Approach

- *Foundation:* Assumes that the market value of a property is closely related to the cost of constructing a substitute property with the same utility.
- *Application:* Often applied to new constructions, special-purpose buildings, schools, churches, and properties not frequently exchanged in the market.

Components of the Cost Approach

Land Value: The first step is determining the value of the vacant land as if it were not improved. This can be estimated through the sales comparison approach for land sales or by extracting land value from sales of improved properties.

Cost of Construction: Estimate the current cost to construct a building or improvement on the property. This includes direct costs (materials and labor) and indirect costs (permits, fees, and overhead).

Depreciation: Subtract depreciation from the total cost of the building. Depreciation accounts for physical wear and tear, functional obsolescence (outdated design or layout), and external obsolescence (loss in value due to external factors like a change in zoning laws).

Calculating Depreciation

- *Physical Depreciation:* Calculated based on the age and condition of the building.
- *Functional Obsolescence:* Estimated by the cost to cure or modify the design flaws or outdated features.
- *External Obsolescence:* Often determined by analyzing similar properties in the area affected by the same external factors.

Formula for the Cost Approach

Value = Land Value + (Replacement Cost New - Depreciation)

Advantages and Limitations

Advantages:

- Provides a clear framework for valuation, especially for new or unique properties.
- Useful for insurance and taxation purposes, where replacement cost is relevant.

Limitations:

- Estimating accurate construction costs and depreciation can be challenging.
- Less applicable to older properties where depreciation is harder to quantify.
- May not always reflect market realities, especially if the property's highest and best use has changed.

The Cost Approach is a vital tool in the appraiser's toolbox, especially for properties that do not generate income or lack comparable sales. Understanding how to accurately assess land value, replacement cost, and depreciation is crucial for applying this approach effectively. While it has its challenges, especially in accurately determining depreciation, the Cost Approach offers a unique perspective on value, particularly for new construction or special-use properties.

Practice Exercise:

Calculate the value of a property using the Cost Approach. Assume you have a parcel of land valued at $100,000. The replacement cost of the building is estimated at $300,000. The building is 10 years old and has an estimated physical depreciation of $50,000, functional obsolescence of $20,000, and no external obsolescence.

Value = Land Value + (Replacement Cost New - Depreciation)

Value = $100,000 + ($300,000 - $70,000

Value = $330,000

This exercise demonstrates how to apply the Cost Approach by breaking down the components and calculating the property value considering the cost of the land, replacement cost of the building, and depreciation factors.

Expanding on the **Income Analysis Approach** to real estate valuation provides a critical perspective on properties as investments, focusing on their potential to generate income. This approach is particularly relevant for commercial, rental, and any income-producing properties, evaluating their worth based on the income they can generate.

Income Analysis Approach

The Income Analysis Approach assesses a property's value based on the income it produces, converting future income into a present value. This method is especially useful for investors and appraisers focusing on properties that generate rental income, such as apartment buildings, office spaces, and retail locations.

Key Concepts

1. Net Operating Income (NOI): The annual income generated by the property after deducting operating expenses but before mortgage payments and taxes. NOI is a crucial figure in the Income Analysis Approach, providing the baseline for determining value.

NOI = Gross Rental Income - Operating Expenses

2. Capitalization Rate (Cap Rate): A rate that helps in estimating the investor's potential return on investment. It's calculated by dividing the NOI by the property's current market value or selling price.

Cap Rate = NOI / Property Value

3. Gross Rent Multiplier (GRM): Offers a simpler, quicker way to estimate property value based on rental income, calculated by dividing the property price by the annual rental income.

GRM = Property Price / Annual Rental Income

4. Gross Income Multiplier (GIM): Similar to GRM but uses gross income, which includes all income from the property, not just rent.

GIM = Property Price / Gross Annual Income

Application of the Income Analysis Approach

- ***Determining Value:*** By understanding the income a property generates, investors can determine a fair value for the property based on expected returns.

- ***Investment Analysis:*** The approach helps in comparing different properties, assessing their profitability and risk, and making informed investment decisions.

Challenges and Considerations

- ***Accurate Income and Expense Reporting:*** Ensuring that all potential income streams are accounted for and that expenses are accurately estimated is vital for a reliable valuation.

- ***Market Cap Rate Comparisons:*** The cap rate must reflect the current market conditions and expectations for the type of property being appraised, requiring knowledge of local and broader market trends.

- ***Lease Terms and Vacancy Rates:*** Understanding the terms of current leases and the typical vacancy rates for similar properties in the area can significantly impact the valuation.

The Income Analysis Approach provides a direct link between a property's value and its ability to generate income, making it an essential tool for investors and appraisers alike. By meticulously analyzing NOI, cap rates, GRM, and GIM, stakeholders can make well-informed decisions regarding property investments. This approach emphasizes the importance of detailed financial analysis and market research in the valuation process.

Practice Exercise:

Consider a multi-family property with an annual gross rental income of $120,000 and operating expenses of $30,000. The local cap rate for similar properties is 5%.

1. Calculate the NOI.

2. Determine the property's value using the cap rate.

Solutions:

1. NOI Calculation:

NOI = $120,000 - $30,000 = $90,000

2. Property Value Calculation:

Property Value = NOI/Cap Rate = $90,000/0.05 = $1,800,000

Capitalization Rate (Cap Rate)

The **Cap Rate** is a key tool in the Income Analysis Approach, offering a method to evaluate the return on investment for income-producing properties. It's particularly useful for real estate investors comparing the potential yield of various properties. The Cap Rate helps translate the income generated by the property into an estimate of the property's overall value, providing a snapshot of its performance independent of the buyer's financing.

Formula:

Cap Rate = NOI / Property Value

Application:

- Ideal for investors focusing on commercial real estate.
- Allows comparison across different markets and property types.
- Sensitive to changes in NOI and market conditions, requiring up-to-date data for accuracy.

Comparative Market Analysis (CMA)

While the *Comparative Market Analysis (CMA)* wasn't explicitly covered in the detailed explanation of the Income Analysis Approach, it's another pivotal valuation method, primarily used in residential real estate to estimate a home's market value. It involves comparing the subject property with similar properties that have recently sold, are currently listed, or were listed but did not sell within a reasonably close proximity.

Key Elements:
- Selection of comparable properties ("comps") with similar characteristics.
- Adjustments for differences in size, condition, location, and features.
- Analysis of current market trends affecting supply and demand.

Purpose:
- Help sellers set listing prices and buyers make competitive offers.
- Provide market insights for appraisers and real estate agents.

Each valuation approach—whether it's the Income Analysis Approach with its focus on income generation and Cap Rates, or the Comparative Market Analysis with its emphasis on comparing sales—plays a vital role in real estate valuation. These methods can be used independently or together to provide a comprehensive view of a property's value, depending on the property type, available data, and the purpose of the valuation.

Reconciliation - A Final Estimate of Value

Reconciliation in real estate appraisal is the process of analyzing and integrating the results obtained from different valuation approaches to establish a final estimate of a property's market value. This critical step ensures a comprehensive evaluation, considering multiple perspectives and reducing the margin of error inherent in any single method.

Purpose of Reconciliation

- *Accuracy:* Combines insights from different approaches to enhance the accuracy of the valuation.
- *Confidence:* Provides a more reliable basis for decision-making by reconciling differing value indications.
- *Compliance:* Meets the professional standards and guidelines required in formal appraisals.

Process of Reconciliation

1. Review of Approaches: Start with a thorough review of the results from the Sales Comparison, Cost, and Income Analysis Approaches, noting the strengths and limitations of each in the context of the subject property.

2. Analysis of Data Consistency: Evaluate the consistency of data and assumptions across the approaches. Significant discrepancies may require a revisit to the underlying data or assumptions for accuracy.

3. Adjustment for Relevance: Give weight to the valuation approach most relevant to the property type and purpose of the appraisal. For instance, the Income Analysis Approach may hold more weight for an investment property, while the Sales Comparison Approach might be more relevant for a residential property.

4. Consideration of Market Trends: Integrate current market trends and future projections that might impact the property's value. This includes economic conditions, interest rates, and local market supply and demand dynamics.

5. Final Value Determination: Synthesize the findings to arrive at a final value estimate. This involves judgment and expertise to balance the quantitative outcomes with qualitative insights about the property and market.

Challenges in Reconciliation

- *Subjectivity:* Despite being data-driven, reconciliation involves subjective judgment, requiring expertise and experience.
- *Market Volatility:* Rapid changes in the market can complicate the reconciliation process, affecting the reliability of the data used in different approaches.
- *Complex Properties:* Unique or special-purpose properties may present challenges in applying standard valuation approaches, complicating the reconciliation process.

Best Practices for Effective Reconciliation

- *Documentation:* Clearly document the rationale behind the weighting and adjustments made during the reconciliation process.
- *Transparency:* Maintain transparency in how different value indications are reconciled, providing confidence in the final estimate.
- *Continuous Learning:* Stay updated with market trends, valuation techniques, and professional standards to enhance the quality of reconciliation.

Reconciliation is a nuanced and critical phase in the valuation process, where the appraiser's skill in analyzing data, understanding market dynamics, and applying professional judgment comes to the forefront. The final estimate of value represents a comprehensive assessment, encapsulating diverse aspects of the property's potential value. Through meticulous reconciliation, appraisers provide stakeholders with a reliable and defensible valuation, essential for informed decision-making in real estate transactions.

Practice Exam 1 : Valuing Real Estate

Instructions:

Select the correct answer for each question. This exam focuses on the mathematical aspects of valuing real estate, including formulas and calculations related to various valuation methods.

1. If a property's annual gross rental income is $120,000 and the asking price is $1,200,000, what is the Gross Rent Multiplier (GRM)?

A) 10

B) 12

C) 100

D) 120

2. A property sold for $400,000. Comparable properties have sold for $390,000, $410,000, and $415,000. What is the average sale price of the comparables?

A) $405,000

B) $403,333

C) $401,667

D) $408,000

3. Using the Cost Approach, if the land is valued at $100,000, the replacement cost of the building is $500,000, and depreciation is estimated at $200,000, what is the property value?

A) $400,000

B) $600,000

C) $700,000

D) $300,000

4. An apartment building generates a Net Operating Income (NOI) of $75,000. If the capitalization rate (Cap Rate) is 7.5%, what is the value of the property?

A) $1,000,000

B) $750,000

C) $1,500,000

D) $1,250,000

5. If the Gross Income Multiplier (GIM) is 8 and the annual gross income is $100,000, what is the value of the property?

A) $800,000

B) $1,250,000

C) $12,500

D) $125,000

6. A commercial property with a NOI of $100,000 is being sold. If similar properties offer a Cap Rate of 8%, what is the market value of the property?

A) $800,000

B) $1,250,000

C) $1,200,000

D) $1,000,000

7. During a Comparative Market Analysis (CMA), a real estate agent adjusts a comp for a $10,000 feature that the subject property does not have. If the comp sold for $310,000, what adjusted sale price should be used for the comparison?

A) $320,000

B) $300,000

C) $310,000

D) $300,000

8. For a property appraisal, three different valuation approaches yielded the following estimates: $250,000 (Sales Comparison), $245,000 (Cost Approach), and $255,000 (Income Approach). If equal weight is given to each approach, what is the reconciled final estimate of value?

A) $250,000

B) $248,333

C) $253,333

D) $247,000

9. A property's operating expenses are $40,000 annually, and it generates $120,000 in rental income each year. What is its Net Operating Income (NOI)?

A) $80,000

B) $160,000

C) $120,000

D) $40,000

10. A retail property is purchased for $2,500,000 and generates an annual NOI of $200,000. What is the Cap Rate?

A) 8%

B) 10%

C) 12%

D) 5%

11. If a property has a GRM of 9.5 and its annual rent is $95,000, what is the estimated property value?

A) $902,500

B) $855,000

C) $1,000,000

D) $905,000

12. The replacement cost of a building is $600,000, and the total depreciation from all sources is estimated at $150,000. If the land value is $200,000, what is the property value according to the Cost Approach?

A) $650,000

B) $750,000

C) $850,000

D) $550,000

13. A multifamily property's GIM is 12, and the gross annual income is projected at $150,000. What is the value of the property?

A) $1,800,000

B) $1,500,000

C) $2,000,000

D) $1,750,000

14. To calculate the Cap Rate, which formula is correct?

A) Cap Rate = Property Value / NOI

B) Cap Rate = NOI / Property Value

C) Cap Rate = Gross Rent / Property Value

D) Cap Rate = Property Value / Gross Rent

15. For a property appraised using the Sales Comparison Approach with three comps sold at $200,000, $210,000, and $190,000 after adjustments, what is the average sale price used for valuation?

A) $200,000

B) $210,000

C) $195,000

D) $600,000

16. A commercial building with an annual gross income of $250,000 and operating expenses of $50,000 is appraised using a Cap Rate of 6.5%. What is the estimated value of the property?

A) $3,076,923
B) $3,800,000
C) $4,000,000
D) $3,500,000

17. If an investment property's GRM is found to be 11 based on market comparisons, and its annual gross rents are $110,000, what would be its approximate market value?

A) $1,100,000
B) $1,210,000
C) $12,100
D) $1,000,000

18. In a reconciliation process, if the Sales Comparison Approach suggests a value of $300,000, the Cost Approach suggests $310,000, and the Income Approach suggests $295,000, what is a reasonable final estimate if the Sales Comparison Approach is considered most reliable for this residential property?

A) $305,000
B) $301,667
C) $300,000
D) $310,000

19. A building generates $120,000 in annual net operating income. If similar buildings are selling at a Cap Rate of 10%, what is the building's value?

A) $1,200,000

B) $1,000,000

C) $12,000,000

D) $1,500,000

20. The cost to construct a new building is $500,000, land value is $200,000, and accumulated depreciation is $100,000. What is the total property value using the Cost Approach?

A) $600,000

B) $700,000

C) $800,000

D) $500,000

Correct Answers for Practice Exam 1 - Valuing Real Estate

1. A) 10

2. B) $403,333

3. A) $400,000

4. C) $1,000,000

5. A) $800,000

6. B) $1,250,000

7. D) $300,000

8. B) $250,000

9. A) $80,000

10. A) 8%

11. A) $902,500

12. B) $750,000

13. A) $1,800,000

14. B) NOI / Property Value

15. A) $200,000

16. A) $3,076,923

17. B) $1,210,000

18. C) $300,000

19. A) $1,200,000

20. A) $600,000

Practice Exam 2: Valuing Real Estate

Instructions:

Select the correct answer for each question. This exam combines mathematical calculations with theoretical knowledge to evaluate understanding of real estate valuation concepts.

1. What is the GRM if a property valued at $950,000 generates an annual rental income of $95,000?

A) 10
B) 9.5
C) 11
D) 8.5

2. If three comparable properties sold for $200,000, $210,000, and $205,000, what is the average sale price?

A) $205,000
B) $215,000
C) $207,500
D) $208,333

3. Which factor is NOT typically adjusted for in the Sales Comparison Approach?

A) Color of the house
B) Size of the property
C) Location
D) Number of bedrooms

4. A building with a replacement cost of $800,000 and accrued depreciation of $300,000 sits on land worth $200,000. Using the Cost Approach, what is the value of the property?

A) $700,000

B) $500,000

C) $1,000,000

D) $1,300,000

5. What is the NOI of a property that generates $120,000 in rental income and has $20,000 in operating expenses?

A) $100,000

B) $140,000

C) $120,000

D) $90,000

6. For a property with an NOI of $60,000 and a Cap Rate of 6%, what is the estimated property value?

A) $1,000,000

B) $900,000

C) $1,200,000

D) $1,500,000

7. Which approach to valuation would most likely be used for a public library building?

A) Income Analysis Approach
B) Sales Comparison Approach
C) Cost Approach
D) GRM

8. If a property's GIM is 12 and its gross annual income is $120,000, what is the property's value?

A) $1,440,000
B) $1,200,000
C) $10,000
D) $144,000

9. In reconciliation, if the Sales Comparison Approach values a property at $300,000, the Cost Approach at $310,000, and the Income Approach at $295,000, what is a reasonable final estimate if the property is income-generating?

A) $301,667
B) $300,000
C) $295,000
D) $310,000

10. A property's annual gross income is $150,000, with operating expenses of $30,000. The local average Cap Rate for similar properties is 8%. What is the value of the property?

A) $1,500,000

B) $1,875,000

C) $2,000,000

D) $1,650,000

11. How does external obsolescence affect property value in the Cost Approach?

A) It increases value due to historical significance.

B) It does not affect the property value.

C) It reduces value due to factors outside the property's control.

D) It is considered a physical deterioration.

12. What is the adjusted price of a comp that sold for $350,000 but has one less bathroom than the subject property, assuming the value of a bathroom is estimated at $15,000?

A) $335,000

B) $365,000

C) $350,000

D) $345,000

13. A duplex generates $24,000 in annual rental income. If the market GRM for similar properties is 12, what is the duplex's estimated value?

A) $288,000

B) $200,000

C) $24,000

D) $2,880

14. The replacement cost of an office building is estimated at $2 million, the land value is $500,000, and the total depreciation from all sources is $600,000. What is the building's value using the Cost Approach?

A) $1,900,000

B) $2,500,000

C) $1,400,000

D) $2,100,000

15. When performing a Comparative Market Analysis (CMA), why are recent sales within the neighborhood important?

A) They reflect the current market trends and property demand.

B) They are only important for historical comparison.

C) They determine the physical depreciation rate.

D) They are used to calculate the GRM.

16. A retail space has an annual gross income of $200,000 and expenses totaling $50,000. If the Cap Rate is 5%, what is the estimated property value?

A) $3,000,000
B) $4,000,000
C) $2,500,000
D) $3,500,000

17. An apartment building sold for $1,200,000 with an annual gross rent of $120,000. What is its GRM?

A) 10
B) 12
C) 8
D) 15

18. If a property appraisal considers both the Income Approach and the Cost Approach, which scenario would lead to greater emphasis on the Income Approach?

A) The property is a unique historic home.
B) The property is a newly constructed shopping center.
C) The property is a rental apartment complex.
D) The property is owner-occupied residential land.

19. A commercial building generates $80,000 NOI and is valued at $1,000,000. What is the Cap Rate?

A) 8%
B) 7.5%
C) 10%
D) 12%

20. In the reconciliation process, if an appraiser gives more weight to the Sales Comparison Approach due to abundant market data, what does this imply about the property?

A) It is likely a special-purpose property.

B) It is primarily valued for its income potential.

C) It is similar to many other properties in the area.

D) It lacks comparable sales data.

Correct Answers for Practice Exam 2 - Valuing Real Estate

1. A) 10

2. D) $208,333

3. A) Color of the house

4. A) $700,000

5. A) $100,000

6. A) $1,000,000

7. C) Cost Approach

8. A) $1,440,000

9. B) $300,000

10. B) $1,875,000

11. C) It reduces value due to factors outside the property's control.

12. B) $365,000

13. A) $288,000

14. C) $1,400,000

15. A) They reflect the current market trends and property demand.

16. A) $3,000,000

17. A) 10

18. C) The property is a rental apartment complex.

19. A) 8%

20. C) It is similar to many other properties in the area.

Practice Exam 3: Advanced Valuing Real Estate

Instructions:

Choose the correct answer for each question. This exam combines advanced knowledge-based questions with mathematical problems in real estate valuation, introducing new scenarios and calculations.

1. Which type of depreciation is irrecoverable through property improvements?

A) Physical depreciation

B) Functional obsolescence

C) External obsolescence

D) Economic depreciation

2. A four-unit rental property generates $10,000 per unit in annual gross rent. If the market GRM for similar properties is 8, what is the property's estimated value?

A) $320,000

B) $400,000

C) $800,000

D) $1,200,000

3. What does a Comparative Market Analysis primarily evaluate?

A) Construction costs

B) Rental income potential

C) Comparable sales

D) Replacement cost

4. If a property's Cap Rate increases, what happens to its market value, assuming constant NOI?

A) Increases
B) Decreases
C) Remains the same
D) Doubles

5. Calculating a property's value using the Income Approach, what is the value if it has an NOI of $50,000 and the prevailing cap rate is 5%?

A) $250,000
B) $1,000,000
C) $2,500,000
D) $500,000

6. In the Sales Comparison Approach, if a comparable property sold for $500,000 but had an additional bathroom valued at $20,000, what is the adjusted sale price for comparison?

A) $480,000
B) $500,000
C) $520,000
D) $420,000

7. Which valuation approach is best suited for a newly constructed property with no rental history?

A) Cost Approach
B) Income Approach
C) Sales Comparison Approach
D) Capitalization Rate

8. For a commercial property with $200,000 in annual operating expenses and a gross income of $500,000, what is the NOI?

A) $300,000
B) $200,000
C) $700,000
D) $500,000

9. How is the Gross Income Multiplier (GIM) used in valuing a property?

A) By dividing the property value by the annual gross income
B) By multiplying the gross income by the property's square footage
C) By dividing the annual gross income by the property value
D) By applying it to the net operating income

10. A property appraisal using the Reconciliation Approach gives twice as much weight to the Income Approach as to the Sales Comparison and Cost Approaches. If the Income Approach estimates $600,000, Sales Comparison $580,000, and Cost Approach $590,000, what is the reconciled value?

A) $590,000
B) $592,500
C) $595,000
D) $600,000

11. What factor might cause an appraiser to adjust a comp in the Sales Comparison Approach for a residential property?

A) Proximity to a commercial area
B) Color scheme of the interior
C) Personal property included in the sale
D) Seasonal variations

12. A retail space with a GRM of 12 generates $120,000 in annual rent. What is the estimated property value?

A) $1,440,000
B) $1,000,000
C) $1,200,000
D) $960,000

13. Which condition does NOT typically affect the Gross Rent Multiplier (GRM) of a property?

A) The economic vacancy rate

B) The age of the property

C) The interest rate environment

D) The zoning laws

14. The replacement cost of a residential building is $400,000, land value is $100,000, and accumulated depreciation is estimated at $50,000. Using the Cost Approach, what is the property's value?

A) $450,000

B) $500,000

C) $550,000

D) $400,000

15. What does the term "highest and best use" imply in real estate valuation?

A) The use that will generate the most income regardless of zoning

B) The use that complies with zoning laws and is physically possible

C) The use that will bring the highest sale price in the current market

D) The use that is most desirable to the property owner

16. A property with an annual NOI of $120,000 is for sale in a market where the typical Cap Rate is 10%. What is the implied value of the property?

A) $1,200,000

B) $12,000,000

C) $1,000,000

D) $1,500,000

17. If adjusting a comp for a superior feature that the subject property lacks, which of the following is a correct step?

A) Increase the comp's sale price to match the feature's value

B) Decrease the comp's sale price by the value of the missing feature

C) No adjustment is necessary for superior features

D) Increase the subject property's estimated value by the feature's value

18. What is a critical step in performing a Comparative Market Analysis (CMA) for a residential property?

A) Estimating the replacement cost

B) Calculating the gross income multiplier

C) Identifying comparable recently sold properties

D) Determining the depreciation rate

19. In the Income Approach, if a property's adjusted gross income is expected to grow at 2% annually, how does this affect its valuation?

A) Decreases value due to increased expenses

B) Increases value due to higher future income

C) No impact, as the Cap Rate remains constant

D) Decreases value, as higher income means higher taxes

20. The term "reconciliation" in real estate appraisal refers to:

A) Resolving disputes between buyer and seller over property value

B) Combining different valuation methods to arrive at a final estimate

C) Adjusting property taxes based on new appraisals

D) Re-evaluating a property after significant market changes

Correct Answers for Practice Exam 3 - Valuing Real Estate

1. C) External obsolescence

2. A) $320,000

3. C) Comparable sales

4. B) Decreases

5. B) $1,000,000

6. A) $480,000

7. A) Cost Approach

8. A) $300,000

9. C) By dividing the annual gross income by the property value

10. B) $592,500

11. A) Proximity to a commercial area

12. A) $1,440,000

13. D) The zoning laws

14. A) $450,000

15. B) The use that complies with zoning laws and is physically possible

16. A) $1,200,000

17. B) Decrease the comp's sale price by the value of the missing feature

18. C) Identifying comparable recently sold properties

19. B) Increases value due to higher future income

20. B) Combining different valuation methods to arrive at a final estimate

Real Estate Financing

Real estate financing plays a pivotal role in the home buying process, offering various mechanisms for borrowers to secure funding for their property purchases. Understanding the intricacies of mortgages, interest rates, and financial ratios is crucial for both buyers and real estate professionals. This chapter delves into fundamental concepts of real estate financing, including loan structures, payment calculations, and insurance requirements.

Loan-to-Value (LTV) Ratio

The Loan-to-Value (LTV) ratio is a critical financial metric used in the real estate industry to assess the risk associated with lending money for a mortgage. It compares the size of the loan to the appraised value of the property. This ratio is a key determinant in the lending process, influencing loan approval decisions, interest rates, and the need for Private Mortgage Insurance (PMI).

Calculation of LTV Ratio

The LTV ratio is calculated by dividing the amount of the mortgage loan by the appraised value or purchase price of the property, whichever is less, and then multiplying by 100 to express the ratio as a percentage.

LTV Ratio = (Amount of Loan / Appraised Value of Property) x 100%

Example Calculation:

If a borrower takes out a loan of $180,000 to purchase a home valued at $225,000, the LTV ratio would be:

LTV = (180,000 / 225,000) x 100% = 80%

Importance of LTV Ratio

- *Risk Assessment:* Lenders use the LTV ratio to gauge the risk of lending. A higher LTV ratio indicates higher risk because it means the borrower is financing a larger portion of the property's value.
- *Interest Rates:* Typically, a lower LTV ratio results in more favorable interest rates because it signifies a lower risk to the lender.
- *PMI Requirement:* Borrowers with an LTV ratio higher than 80% usually need to purchase Private Mortgage Insurance, which protects the lender in case of default.

Factors Affecting LTV Ratio

- *Down Payment:* A larger down payment results in a lower LTV ratio, reducing the lender's risk and often improving the loan terms for the borrower.
- *Property Appraisal:* The appraised value of the property can significantly impact the LTV ratio. If the appraisal comes in lower than the purchase price, the LTV ratio increases unless the borrower increases their down payment.

LTV Ratio and Refinancing

When refinancing a mortgage, the LTV ratio is calculated using the current balance of the mortgage and the current appraised value of the property. A lower LTV ratio is beneficial for refinancing as well, potentially qualifying the borrower for lower rates and better terms.

LTV Ratio and Loan Approval

The LTV ratio is a key factor in the loan approval process. Lenders typically have maximum LTV ratio limits based on the loan type and the borrower's credit profile. Loans with higher LTV ratios are seen as riskier and may require additional scrutiny or guarantees.

The Loan-to-Value ratio is a cornerstone of mortgage lending, encapsulating the relationship between the loan amount, the property value, and the inherent risk to the lender. Understanding the LTV ratio helps borrowers navigate the financing process, potentially securing better terms and avoiding the extra cost of PMI with a substantial down payment. It serves as a reminder of the importance of equity and financial planning in real estate transactions.

Practice Exercise:

Calculate the LTV ratio for a borrower who wants to purchase a home with a sale price of $300,000. The borrower has saved $60,000 for a down payment. Determine if PMI would be required based on an 80% threshold for the LTV ratio.

$$\textbf{LTV Ratio} = \left(\frac{300,000 - 60,000}{300,000} \right) \textbf{ x 100\%} = \textbf{80\%}$$

Since the LTV ratio is 80%, the borrower is right at the threshold where PMI may not be required, assuming the lender adheres to common PMI requirements.

Mortgage Points and Calculating Mortgage Payments

Understanding mortgage points and how to calculate mortgage payments are essential aspects of securing a home loan. Mortgage points, often known as discount points, are fees paid upfront to reduce the interest rate on a loan, saving money over the life of the mortgage. Calculating mortgage payments, on the other hand, involves understanding the components that make up the monthly payment.

Mortgage Points

- *Definition:* One mortgage point equals 1% of the loan amount. Paying points lowers the interest rate on your mortgage, which can result in significant savings over time.
- *Benefits:* Lower monthly payments and less interest paid over the life of the loan.

- Considerations: Whether to pay points depends on how long you plan to keep the loan. The longer you keep the loan, the more you save by paying points upfront.

Example:

If you have a $200,000 loan and pay 2 points, you're paying $4,000 upfront. If paying these points lowers your rate from 4.5% to 4.0%, you need to calculate whether the monthly savings will exceed the upfront cost over your expected time in the home.

Calculating Mortgage Payments

The monthly mortgage payment can be calculated using the formula:

$$P = L \frac{c(1+c)^n}{(1+c)^n - 1}$$

Where:
- **P** is the monthly payment
- **L** is the loan amount
- **c** is the monthly interest rate (annual rate divided by 12)
- **n** is the number of payments (loan term in years multiplied by 12)

Components of Mortgage Payments:
- *Principal:* The portion of the payment that reduces the remaining balance of the mortgage.
- *Interest:* The cost of borrowing the principal amount, calculated at the interest rate.
- *Taxes and Insurance:* Often included in monthly payments and held in an escrow account. Not directly included in the formula but essential for calculating the total monthly payment (PITI).

Example Calculation:

For a $200,000 loan at a 4% annual interest rate with a 30-year term:
- Monthly interest rate (c) = 4% / 12 = 0.0033

- Number of payments (n) = 30 * 12 = 360

$$P = 200,000 \, \frac{0.0033 \, (1 + 0.0033)^{360}}{(1 + 0.0033)^{360} - 1}$$

This formula will give you the monthly payment amount that consists solely of principal and interest.

Mortgage points and the calculation of mortgage payments are integral to planning and managing home financing. Points can offer long-term savings on interest, but their value depends on the individual's financial situation and housing goals. Understanding how to calculate your monthly mortgage payment helps in budgeting and making informed decisions about how much home you can afford. By carefully considering these factors, borrowers can optimize their mortgage financing to suit their long-term financial health.

Practice Exercise:

Calculate the monthly payment (principal and interest only) for a $250,000 mortgage at a 3.5% interest rate over a 30-year term. Determine the impact if the borrower decides to pay 1 point upfront to reduce the rate to 3.25%.

- First, calculate the monthly payment with the original rate.
- Then, calculate the cost of 1 point.
- Finally, calculate the new monthly payment with the reduced rate and compare to determine the savings.

To complete the practice exercise, let's calculate the monthly mortgage payment for a $250,000 loan at a 3.5% interest rate over a 30-year term, then determine the impact of paying 1 point (1% of the loan amount) to reduce the rate to 3.25%.

Initial Calculation with a 3.5% Interest Rate

- **Loan Amount (L):** $250,000
- **Annual Interest Rate:** 3.5%
- **Loan Term:** 30 years

First, convert the annual interest rate to a monthly rate by dividing by 12.

- **Monthly Interest Rate (c): 3.5% / 12 = 0.2917%**

Convert the percentage to a decimal for calculation:

c = 0.002917

The number of monthly payments (n) is:

n = 30 x 12 = 360

Using the mortgage payment formula:

$$P = L \frac{c(1+c)^n}{(1+c)^n - 1}$$

$$P = 250,000 \frac{0.002917(1+0.002917)^{360}}{(1+0.002917)^{360} - 1}$$

Calculation with a 3.25% Interest Rate (After Paying 1 Point)

- **Cost of 1 Point:** 1% of $250,000 = $2,500
- **New Annual Interest Rate:** 3.25%
- **Monthly Interest Rate (c):** 3.25% / 12 = 0.2708% or $(c = 0.002708)$

Using the mortgage payment formula with the new rate:

$$P = 250,000 \frac{0.002708(1+0.002708)^{360}}{(1+0.002708)^{360} - 1}$$

The formulas provided above allow for calculating the monthly mortgage payment for both scenarios. The calculations involve complex arithmetic that typically requires a financial calculator or software for exact figures. However, the essence of the calculation is:

- For an interest rate of 3.5%, the formula calculates the monthly payment considering the interest compounding over 360 months.
- After reducing the interest rate to 3.25% by paying 1 point, the monthly payment decreases due to the lower interest rate, despite the same loan amount and term.

- The monthly payment at 3.5% interest was approximately $1,122.61.
- After paying 1 point to reduce the rate to 3.25%, the monthly payment became approximately $1,088.02.
- The savings per month amounted to approximately $34.60.

This demonstrates the financial impact of purchasing points to lower the interest rate. The decision to purchase points should be based on the expected duration of the mortgage and whether the upfront cost is justified by the long-term savings.

Amortization and Amortization Schedule

Amortization in the context of a mortgage refers to the process of paying off debt over time through regular payments. The payments cover both the principal (the original loan amount) and the interest accrued. An amortization schedule, on the other hand, is a detailed table that outlines how each payment is allocated between principal and interest and shows the remaining balance after each payment.

Understanding Amortization

- *Principle:* Early in the loan term, a larger portion of each payment is applied to interest. As the loan matures, more of each payment goes toward reducing the principal.
- *Benefits:* Amortization provides a clear path to becoming debt-free within a specified period. For borrowers, it offers predictability and a structured repayment plan.

Amortization Schedule Components

Payment Date: When each payment is due.

Payment Amount: The total amount paid in each period, typically monthly.

Principal Portion: The part of the payment that reduces the loan balance.

Interest Portion: The part of the payment that covers the interest on the loan.

Remaining Balance: The loan balance after each payment is made.

Calculating an Amortization Schedule

To create an amortization schedule, you need the loan amount, the interest rate, the term of the loan, and the payment frequency. The schedule is calculated by:

Determining the Monthly Payment: Using the formula provided in the mortgage payment calculation section.

Calculating Interest for the Period: Multiply the current balance by the periodic interest rate.

Applying Payment to Interest and Principal: Subtract the interest portion from the total payment to determine the amount applied to the principal.

Updating the Balance: Subtract the principal portion from the current balance to find the new balance.

Example:

For a $200,000 loan at a 4% annual interest rate with a 30-year term:

- The monthly payment, calculated using the formula, might be approximately $955 (for principal and interest).

- In the first month, the interest portion would be $666.67 ($200,000 x 4% / 12), and the principal portion would be $288.33 ($955 - $666.67).

- The new balance after the first payment would be $199,711.67 ($200,000 - $288.33).

Importance of Amortization for Borrowers

Over time, as more of the payment goes toward the principal, the borrower's equity in the property increases.

Making additional principal payments can accelerate amortization, reducing the total interest paid over the life of the loan.

Amortization is a fundamental concept in real estate financing, providing borrowers with a systematic approach to debt repayment. An amortization schedule not only helps in tracking payments and outstanding balances but also in planning for prepayments or refinancing. Understanding how each payment is split between principal and interest can empower borrowers to make informed financial decisions regarding their mortgages.

Practice Exercise:

Create a simple amortization schedule for the first year of a $100,000 mortgage at a 5% annual interest rate with a 30-year term. Calculate the monthly payment, then break down the first 12 payments into interest and principal components, updating the balance each month.

This exercise will enhance understanding of how payments are allocated in the early stages of a mortgage and the effect on the loan balance.

Now, to solve the practice exercise, we'll create a simple amortization schedule for the first year of a $100,000 mortgage at a 5% annual interest rate with a 30-year term. We need to calculate the monthly payment first, then break down the first 12 payments into interest and principal components.

Step 1: Calculate the Monthly Payment

The formula for calculating the monthly mortgage payment is:

$$P = L \frac{c(1+c)^n}{(1+c)^n - 1}$$

Where:

- **P** is the monthly payment
- **L** is the loan amount ($100,000)
- **c** is the monthly interest rate (annual rate / 12 months, in decimal form)
- **n** is the number of payments (loan term in years * 12)

Given:

- L = 100,000
- Annual interest rate = 5% (0.05 in decimal form)
- Monthly interest rate = 0.05 / 12 = 0.0041667
- n = 30 x 12 = 360

Plugging the values into the formula gives us:

$$P = 100,000 \frac{0.0041667(1+0.0041667)^{360}}{(1+0.0041667)^{360} - 1}$$

Step 2: Monthly Payment Calculation

P ≈ 536.82

This is the monthly payment for principal and interest.

Step 3: Amortization Schedule for the First Year

For each month, we calculate:

- **Interest for the period:** Current balance x monthly interest rate
- **Principal portion:** Monthly payment – interest portion
- **New balance:** Previous balance – principal portion

Month 1:

- **Interest:** $100,000 x 0.0041667 = $416.67

- **Principal:** $536.82 − $416.67 = $120.15

- **New Balance:** $100,000 − $120.15 = $99,879.85

Following this method, let's calculate the interest, principal, and new balance for the next couple of months to illustrate the process:

Month 2:

- **Interest:** $99,879.85 x 0.0041667 ≈ $416.16

- **Principal:** $536.82 − $416.16 ≈ $120.66

- **New Balance:** $99,879.85 − $120.66 ≈ $99,759.19

Month 3:

- **Interest:** $99,759.19 x 0.0041667 ≈ $415.65

- **Principal:** $536.82 − $415.65 ≈ $121.17

- **New Balance:** $99,759.19 − $121.17 ≈ $99,638.02

Continuing this process will give you the breakdown for each of the first 12 months. The exercise demonstrates how with each payment, the interest portion decreases, and the principal portion increases, gradually reducing the outstanding loan balance. For brevity, the detailed calculations for the remaining months can follow the same pattern, adjusting for the new balance each time. This exercise underscores the early impact of interest in amortized loans and the gradual increase in equity over time.

Principal, Interest, Taxes, and Insurance (PITI)

Principal, Interest, Taxes, and Insurance (PITI) represent the core components of a typical monthly mortgage payment. Understanding PITI is crucial for homeowners and potential buyers to accurately budget for the total cost of owning a home. Each component plays a significant role in the overall financial commitment involved in a mortgage.

Principal and Interest

- ***Principal:*** The principal portion of the mortgage payment reduces the outstanding balance of the loan. Initially, it's a smaller part of the payment but grows over time due to the amortization schedule.
- ***Interest:*** Interest is the cost of borrowing money, calculated as a percentage of the outstanding loan balance. Earlier in the loan term, the interest portion dominates the monthly payment.

Property Taxes

- ***Taxes:*** Property taxes are levied by local governments and are used to fund public services. The amount is based on the assessed value of the property and the local tax rate.
- ***Payment Method:*** Often, lenders will escrow property taxes, collecting them as part of the monthly mortgage payment and then paying the tax bill on behalf of the homeowner.

Homeowner's Insurance

- ***Insurance:*** Homeowner's insurance protects against loss from damages to the property, covering scenarios like fire, theft, and some natural disasters.
- ***Escrow:*** Like property taxes, insurance premiums are frequently escrowed by the lender, ensuring the policy remains active as a condition of the loan.

Private Mortgage Insurance (PMI)

- When the down payment is less than 20% of the home's purchase price, lenders typically require PMI. This insurance protects the lender in case the borrower defaults on the loan. PMI is included in the monthly payment until the LTV ratio reaches a certain threshold.

Calculating PITI

To calculate the total monthly PITI payment, add together the monthly principal and interest payment (determined by the loan amount, interest rate, and term), the monthly property tax payment (annual tax bill divided by 12), and the monthly homeowner's insurance payment (annual premium divided by 12). If applicable, include PMI as well.

PITI = Principal + Interest + Monthly Property Taxes + Monthly Insurance

Importance of PITI in Mortgage Approval

- *Lenders' Perspective:* Lenders use PITI to determine a borrower's monthly housing expense. This calculation helps assess whether a borrower can afford the loan, based on their income and other debts.
- *Debt-to-Income Ratio:* PITI is factored into the borrower's front-end DTI ratio, a key metric lenders evaluate during the loan approval process.

Budgeting for Homeowners

Understanding PITI is vital for homeowners to budget accurately for the true cost of owning a home. It goes beyond the loan's principal and interest, incorporating taxes and insurance into the financial planning process.

- PITI sums up the comprehensive monthly expense of maintaining a mortgage and owning a home. By fully grasping the components of PITI, prospective homeowners can make informed decisions about affordability, ensuring that they are prepared for the full scope of homeownership costs.

Practice Exercise:

Calculate the monthly PITI payment for a home with a $250,000 mortgage at a 4% interest rate for 30 years, annual property taxes of $3,600, and an annual homeowner's insurance premium of $1,200. Assume no PMI is required.

This exercise will help illustrate how to compile the various expenses into a single, comprehensive monthly payment, offering insights into the total monthly cost of owning a specific property. So let's solve it!

Step 1: Calculate the Monthly Mortgage Payment (Principal and Interest)

Given:

- Loan Amount (L) = $250,000

- Annual Interest Rate (r) = 4% (or 0.04 as a decimal)

- Loan Term = 30 years

First, convert the annual interest rate to a monthly rate (c) and the loan term to months (n):

- c = 0.04/12 = 0.003333

- n = 30 x 12 = 360

The formula for the monthly mortgage payment (P) is:

$$P = L \frac{c(1+c)^n}{(1+c)^n - 1}$$

$$P = 250,000 \frac{0{,}003333\,(1 + 0{,}003333)^{360}}{(1 + 0{,}003333)^{360} - 1}$$

Step 2: Calculate the Monthly Property Taxes

- Annual Property Taxes = $3,600
- Monthly Property Taxes = 3,600 / 12 = $300

Step 3: Calculate the Monthly Homeowner's Insurance Premium

- Annual Homeowner's Insurance = $1,200
- Monthly Insurance = 1,200 / 12 = $100

Step 4: Compile the PITI Payment

The PITI payment is the sum of the monthly principal and interest payment from Step 1, the monthly property taxes from Step 2, and the monthly insurance premium from Step 3. PMI is not included as it's assumed not to be required.

Let's calculate the monthly mortgage payment (P) from Step 1:

$$P \approx 250,000 \, \frac{0{,}003333 \, (1 + 0{,}003333)^{360}}{(1 + 0{,}003333)^{360} - 1} \approx \$1{,}193.54$$

(Note: This calculation is approximated for simplicity.)

Finally, add the monthly property taxes and insurance to the monthly mortgage payment:

- Total PITI Payment = $1,193.54 + $300 + $100 = $1,593.54

Therefore, the monthly PITI payment for this home, under the given conditions, would be approximately $1,593.54. This figure represents the total monthly cost of owning the property, excluding any potential PMI or other fees.

Private Mortgage Insurance (PMI)

Private Mortgage Insurance (PMI) is a type of insurance policy that protects lenders from the risk of default and foreclosure. PMI is required when homebuyers obtain a mortgage with a down payment that is less than 20% of the home's purchase price or appraised value. By providing this insurance, lenders are able to offer loans to borrowers with smaller down payments, thereby increasing homeownership access.

When is PMI Required?

PMI is typically mandated by lenders as part of the loan agreement when the Loan-to-Value (LTV) ratio exceeds 80%. The LTV ratio is a financial term used by lenders to compare the amount of the mortgage loan with the value of the property. An LTV ratio over 80% indicates to the lender that there is an increased risk of loan default, as the borrower has less equity in the property.

Cost of PMI

- The cost of PMI can vary depending on the size of the down payment, the loan terms, and the borrower's credit score. It generally ranges from 0.3% to 1.5% of the original loan amount per year.
- PMI premiums can be paid monthly, as part of the overall mortgage payment, or upfront at closing. Some lenders may offer a combination of both.

Calculating PMI Payments

To calculate the annual PMI cost, you can use the following formula:

Annual PMI Cost = Loan Amount x PMI Rate

For monthly PMI payments, divide the annual PMI cost by 12.

Example:

For a $200,000 loan with a PMI rate of 1%:

Annual PMI Cost = 200,000 x 0.01 = $2,000

Monthly PMI Payment = $2,000/12 ≈ $166.67

Impact of PMI on Borrowers

While PMI enables borrowers to purchase homes with smaller down payments, it represents an additional monthly expense that does not contribute to equity in the home. Borrowers should consider the long-term costs of PMI when deciding how much to put down on a home purchase.

Cancellation of PMI

Borrowers have the right to request the cancellation of PMI once their LTV ratio reaches 78% based on the original value of the property, as long as they are in good standing with their loan payments. Additionally, the Homeowners Protection Act mandates automatic termination of PMI when the LTV ratio is scheduled to reach 78%, irrespective of the current balance, for borrowers in good standing.

So, PMI plays a crucial role in the mortgage industry, allowing individuals to become homeowners without needing to save for a large down payment. However, it's important for borrowers to be aware of the costs associated with PMI and to plan for its eventual cancellation to reduce their overall mortgage expenses. Understanding the specifics of PMI can help borrowers make informed decisions about their home financing options and potentially save thousands of dollars over the life of their loan.

Debt-to-Income (DTI) Ratio

The Debt-to-Income (DTI) Ratio is a key financial metric used by lenders to determine a borrower's ability to manage monthly payments and repay debts. It measures the proportion of a borrower's gross monthly income that goes towards paying debts, including the prospective mortgage, credit card payments, student loans, auto loans, and other debt obligations.

Calculation of DTI Ratio

The DTI ratio is calculated by dividing the total of all monthly debt payments by the borrower's gross monthly income (before taxes and other deductions). The result is expressed as a percentage. There are two main types of DTI ratios considered in mortgage applications:

Front-End DTI Ratio: This ratio considers only housing-related expenses, such as monthly mortgage payments, property taxes, insurance, and homeowners association fees, divided by gross monthly income.

Back-End DTI Ratio: This encompasses all debt obligations per month, including housing expenses and recurring debt payments, divided by gross monthly income.

Formula:

$$\text{DTI Ratio} = \left(\frac{Total\ Monthly\ Debt\ Payments}{Gross\ Monthly\ Income}\right) \times 100\%$$

Example Calculation:

If a borrower has a gross monthly income of $5,000, a monthly mortgage payment of $1,200, and other monthly debt payments totaling $800, the back-end DTI ratio would be:

$$\text{DTI Ratio} = \left(\frac{1200+800}{5000}\right) \times 100\% = 40\%$$

Significance in the Mortgage Process

- *Lender Assessment:* Lenders use the DTI ratio to gauge a borrower's financial health and to assess the risk of lending. A lower DTI ratio indicates a borrower has a good balance between debt and income.
- *Loan Approval:* Generally, lenders prefer a back-end DTI ratio of 36% or lower, though some loan programs allow for higher ratios. The front-end DTI ratio, though less universally specified, is often preferred to be under 28%.

Implications of a High DTI Ratio

A high DTI ratio can be a red flag for lenders, suggesting that a borrower might struggle to manage additional loan payments. It can lead to challenges in securing mortgage approval or result in higher interest rates to mitigate the lender's risk.

Improving Your DTI Ratio

Borrowers can improve their DTI ratio by increasing their income, paying off existing debts, or doing both. Reducing debt not only improves the DTI ratio but also can lead to better loan terms and interest rates.

In conclusion, the DTI ratio is a critical determinant of borrowing capacity in the real estate market. Understanding and optimizing this ratio can greatly enhance a borrower's prospects for loan approval and favorable mortgage terms. By managing debt responsibly and maximizing income, potential homeowners can position themselves as attractive candidates to lenders.

Escrow Accounts

Escrow accounts are a fundamental component of the home buying process, acting as a financial arrangement where a third party holds and regulates payment of the funds required for two parties involved in a given transaction. In the context of real estate financing, lenders often use escrow accounts to manage and disburse funds for property taxes and homeowner's insurance on behalf of the borrower.

Purpose and Functionality

The primary purpose of an escrow account is to ensure that property taxes and insurance premiums are paid on time, protecting the lender's interest in the property. By collecting a portion of these costs with each mortgage payment, lenders accumulate sufficient funds within the escrow account to cover the expenses when they are due.

How Escrow Accounts Work

Initial Setup: When closing on a home loan, the lender may set up an escrow account to collect future payments for taxes and insurance. Sometimes, an initial deposit may be required to start the account.

Monthly Payments: Alongside principal and interest, the borrower pays a portion of the estimated annual costs for property taxes and insurance into the escrow account.

Annual Disbursements: The lender uses the funds in the escrow account to pay the property taxes and insurance premiums when they are due. The lender is responsible for managing the account and ensuring payments are made on time.

Adjustments and Reviews

- *Annual Escrow Analysis:* Lenders conduct an annual review of the escrow account to adjust the monthly payment as needed, based on changes in tax rates or insurance premiums. This ensures that the account holds enough funds to cover the expenses without maintaining a surplus beyond the legal limit.

Benefits of Escrow Accounts

- *Convenience for Borrowers:* Escrow accounts simplify budgeting by incorporating tax and insurance payments into the monthly mortgage payment, ensuring these critical expenses are not overlooked.
- *Protection for Lenders:* By guaranteeing that taxes and insurance are paid on time, escrow accounts reduce the risk of tax liens or uninsured losses that could jeopardize the lender's collateral.

Potential Downsides

- *Lack of Control:* Borrowers have limited control over the escrow account, relying on the lender to make timely payments. Some may prefer managing these payments directly.
- *Fluctuating Payments:* Escrow payments can change yearly based on actual tax and insurance costs, which can lead to unexpected increases in monthly mortgage payments.

Opting Out

In certain cases, borrowers with a low loan-to-value ratio or those who have built up sufficient equity may have the option to waive the escrow requirement and pay taxes and insurance directly. However, this often requires lender approval and might come with increased interest rates or fees due to the perceived increase in risk.

In conclusion, escrow accounts play a crucial role in the mortgage ecosystem, offering benefits in terms of convenience and risk management. While they do come with some trade-offs in terms of direct control over payments, for many homeowners, the advantages of ensuring consistent, on-time payment of taxes and insurance outweigh the drawbacks. Understanding how these accounts work can help borrowers navigate their mortgage payments more effectively, ensuring a smoother homeownership experience.

How Mortgage Interest is Paid

Understanding how mortgage interest is paid is crucial for any homebuyer or homeowner with a mortgage. Mortgage interest is the cost charged by the lender for borrowing money to purchase a home. It is determined by the interest rate of the mortgage and is typically paid alongside the principal loan amount in monthly installments over the life of the loan.

Interest Structure in Mortgage Payments

Mortgage payments are composed of two main parts: the principal, which reduces the loan balance, and the interest, which is the cost of borrowing. In the early years of a mortgage, a larger portion of each monthly payment is allocated to interest due to the amortization process. As the principal balance decreases over time, the interest portion of each payment decreases, while the principal portion increases.

Amortization: The Key to Understanding Interest Payments

- **Amortization** is the process that schedules the gradual reduction of the mortgage loan through monthly payments of principal and interest. This schedule dictates that earlier payments are predominantly interest, with the balance shifting more towards the principal as the loan matures.

Calculating Interest Payments

Interest for each payment period is calculated based on the remaining balance of the loan at the beginning of the period. The formula to calculate the interest portion of a payment is:

Interest Payment = Outstanding Principal Balance x Monthly Interest Rate

The monthly interest rate is derived from the annual interest rate divided by 12.

Impact of Extra Payments

Making extra payments directly towards the principal can significantly alter the amortization schedule, reducing the total interest paid over the life of the loan and potentially shortening the loan term. Extra payments decrease the principal balance faster, thereby reducing the interest calculated in subsequent months.

Interest-Only Mortgages

In contrast to traditional amortizing mortgages, interest-only mortgages require borrowers to pay only the interest for a certain period, after which the payment structure shifts to include both principal and interest. During the interest-only period, no principal is paid down, and the total loan amount remains unchanged.

Fixed-Rate vs. Adjustable-Rate Mortgages

- *Fixed-Rate Mortgages:* The interest rate remains constant throughout the term of the loan, resulting in predictable monthly payments.
- *Adjustable-Rate Mortgages (ARMs):* The interest rate can change at specified times based on market conditions, affecting the amount of interest paid and potentially altering monthly payment amounts.

So, the way mortgage interest is paid is fundamental to understanding the overall cost of a mortgage and how each payment contributes to reducing the loan balance. Borrowers should consider the type of mortgage, the effects of amortization, and the potential benefits of making extra payments towards the principal. Awareness of how interest accumulates and is paid off over time is essential for effective mortgage planning and financial management, ensuring borrowers can make informed decisions to minimize costs and maximize equity in their homes.

Practice Exam 1 : Real Estate Financing

Instructions:

Choose the correct answer for each question. This exam covers essential concepts of real estate financing, including loan-to-value ratios, mortgage calculations, and more.

1. What does the Loan-to-Value (LTV) Ratio represent?

A) The percentage of the loan compared to the seller's asking price

B) The percentage of the loan compared to the appraised property value

C) The interest rate of the mortgage loan

D) The percentage of the property already paid off

2. How are mortgage points primarily used?

A) To increase the loan amount

B) To cover closing costs

C) To reduce the loan's interest rate

D) To extend the loan term

3. What does an amortization schedule show?

A) The increase in property value over time

B) The breakdown of each payment into principal and interest over the loan term

C) The total interest paid over the life of the loan

D) Monthly rental income from the property

4. What are the components of PITI?

A) Principal, Interest, Taxes, Insurance

B) Property, Income, Taxes, Interest

C) Principal, Income, Title, Insurance

D) Property, Interest, Title, Insurance

5. Under what condition is Private Mortgage Insurance (PMI) typically required?

A) When the down payment is less than 10% of the home's purchase price

B) When the down payment is less than 20% of the home's purchase price

C) When the mortgage term is longer than 15 years

D) When purchasing investment property

6. What does the Debt-to-Income (DTI) Ratio measure?

A) The ratio of a borrower's total monthly debt payments to their total monthly income

B) The ratio of a borrower's monthly mortgage payment to their total monthly income

C) The ratio of a borrower's total monthly income to their total monthly debt payments

D) The ratio of a borrower's total monthly mortgage payment to their gross annual income

7. What is the purpose of an escrow account in real estate financing?

A) To hold the borrower's down payment until closing

B) To collect and pay property taxes and insurance premiums on behalf of the homeowner

C) To save for future home repairs

D) To secure the mortgage note

8. How does making extra payments toward the mortgage principal affect interest paid over the life of the loan?

A) Increases the total interest paid

B) Decreases the total interest paid

C) Has no effect on interest paid

D) Only affects the loan term, not the interest paid

9. What happens to the monthly payment if a borrower chooses to pay mortgage points at closing?

A) Increases significantly

B) Decreases due to a lower interest rate

C) Remains the same

D) Increases due to additional loan fees

10. How is the monthly interest portion of a mortgage payment calculated in the early years of the loan?

A) It's a fixed amount determined at closing

B) It decreases each month as the loan balance decreases

C) It constitutes the majority of the monthly payment

D) It's calculated based on the remaining loan balance

11. When can a homeowner request to cancel PMI?

A) Once they have made the first year of payments

B) When the loan balance reaches 78% of the original appraised value

C) After remodeling the home

D) When interest rates drop

12. Which type of interest calculation method results in lower interest costs over the life of the loan?

A) Simple interest

B) Compound interest

C) Daily interest

D) Amortized interest

13. Which factor does NOT directly affect the amount of interest paid over the life of a mortgage?

A) The home's appraised value

B) The loan amount

C) The interest rate

D) The loan term

14. What is the primary advantage of a fixed-rate mortgage over an adjustable-rate mortgage (ARM)?

A) Lower interest rates in the first few years

B) The interest rate and monthly payments remain the same throughout the loan term

C) The ability to convert to a fixed-rate mortgage without refinancing

D) Lower closing costs

15. How does a decrease in the interest rate affect the amortization schedule of a fixed-rate mortgage?

A) Increases the total number of payments

B) Decreases the total number of payments

C) No effect, as the payment schedule is fixed

D) Decreases the amount of each payment

16. What is the effect of a higher LTV ratio on a mortgage application?

A) Lower interest rates

B) Higher interest rates

C) Faster loan approval

D) Automatic loan approval

17. Why might a borrower choose to have an escrow account?

A) To reduce the loan's interest rate

B) To ensure timely payment of property taxes and insurance

C) To avoid paying property taxes

D) To lower the home's purchase price

18. In what scenario would a lender most likely require PMI?

A) The borrower makes a 30% down payment

B) The borrower has an excellent credit score

C) The borrower makes a 15% down payment

D) The mortgage is for a second home

19. How is the front-end DTI ratio different from the back-end DTI ratio?

A) Front-end includes housing costs only; back-end includes all debt obligations

B) Front-end includes all debt obligations; back-end includes housing costs only

C) There is no difference; they are calculated the same way

D) Front-end is used for refinancing; back-end is used for initial mortgages

20. What role does amortization play in a mortgage?

A) It allows borrowers to switch lenders without penalties

B) It determines the property's market value

C) It schedules the loan payments so that the loan is paid off by the end

D) It increases the loan amount annually to account for inflation

Correct Answers For Exam 1 - Real Estate Financing

1. B) The percentage of the loan compared to the appraised property value
2. C) To reduce the loan's interest rate
3. B) The breakdown of each payment into principal and interest over the loan term
4. A) Principal, Interest, Taxes, Insurance
5. B) When the down payment is less than 20% of the home's purchase price
6. A) The ratio of a borrower's total monthly debt payments to their total monthly income
7. B) To collect and pay property taxes and insurance premiums on behalf of the homeowner
8. B) Decreases the total interest paid
9. B) Decreases due to a lower interest rate
10. C) It constitutes the majority of the monthly payment
11. B) When the loan balance reaches 78% of the original appraised value
12. D) Amortized interest
13. A) The home's appraised value
14. B) The interest rate and monthly payments remain the same throughout the loan term
15. C) No effect, as the payment schedule is fixed (Clarification: For a fixed-rate mortgage, changes in interest rates do not affect the payment schedule unless the mortgage is refinanced.)
16. B) Higher interest rates
17. B) To ensure timely payment of property taxes and insurance
18. C) The borrower makes a 15% down payment
19. A) Front-end includes housing costs only; back-end includes all debt obligations
20. C) It schedules the loan payments so that the loan is paid off by the end

Practice Exam 2: Real Estate Financing

Instructions:

Choose the correct answer for each math-focused question related to real estate financing. This exam emphasizes calculations, ratios, and financial concepts integral to understanding and navigating the mortgage process.

1. If a home is purchased for $300,000 with a down payment of 10%, what is the Loan-to-Value (LTV) ratio?

A) 90%

B) 80%

C) 10%

D) 100%

2. How much interest is saved over the life of a loan by paying an upfront fee of 1 mortgage point on a $200,000 loan, if the point reduces the interest rate from 4.5% to 4.25% for a 30-year term? (Assume monthly payments)

A) $10,000

B) $12,500

C) $15,000

D) $9,500

3. Calculate the monthly principal and interest payment (P&I) for a $250,000 mortgage at a 3.5% annual interest rate for 30 years.

A) $1,122.61

B) $1,347.13

C) $1,632.96

D) $1,193.54

4. If property taxes are $4,800 annually and homeowner's insurance is $1,200 annually, what is the monthly PITI payment for the mortgage in question 3?

A) $1,522.61

B) $1,747.13

C) $2,032.96

D) $1,593.54

5. For a loan amount of $180,000 and an annual PMI rate of 0.7%, how much is the monthly PMI payment?

A) $105

B) $126

C) $150

D) $210

6. If a borrower's gross monthly income is $5,000, and their total monthly debt payments including the new mortgage will be $2,000, what is their back-end DTI ratio?

A) 25%

B) 30%

C) 40%

D) 50%

7. How much does a borrower need to pay upfront for escrow at closing if the lender requires two months of property taxes and insurance premiums, based on the annual amounts in question 4?

A) $500
B) $600
C) $1,000
D) $1,200

8. If making an additional annual payment of $1,200 towards the principal reduces the total interest paid by $10,000 over the life of a 30-year loan, what is the initial loan amount, assuming a 4% interest rate?

   - Use question 3's payment for a $250,000 loan at 3.5% as a reference point for calculation estimates.

A) $200,000
B) $220,000
C) $250,000
D) $275,000

9. What is the new monthly mortgage payment after recasting a $200,000 loan balance at 4% interest over the remaining 20 years, if the borrower makes a lump sum payment of $40,000 towards the principal?

A) $1,212
B) $909.12
C) $1,102.22
D) $967.36

10. A borrower refinances their mortgage to a lower interest rate, reducing their monthly payment by $150. If the cost to refinance is $3,600, how many months will it take to break even on the refinancing costs?

A) 24 months

B) 18 months

C) 12 months

D) 30 months

11. If an adjustable-rate mortgage (ARM) starts at 3.5% and can increase up to 2% annually with a cap of 7.5%, what is the maximum possible monthly payment in the third year for a $250,000 loan, assuming it adjusts to the cap as quickly as possible?

A) $1,796.18

B) $1,632.96

C) $1,347.13

D) $1,122.61

12. For a $150,000 loan amount with an LTV of 80%, what is the minimum down payment required?

A) $30,000

B) $37,500

C) $40,000

D) $20,000

13. Calculate the total interest paid over the life of a $300,000 loan at 4% interest for 15 years.

A) $99,431.27
B) $66,287.85
C) $122,748.15
D) $89,528.39

14. How does a yearly increase in property tax from $4,800 to $5,100 affect the monthly PITI payment, assuming the mortgage payment remains constant?

A) Increases by $25
B) Decreases by $25
C) Increases by $50
D) No change

15. A borrower's annual homeowner's insurance premium increases from $1,200 to $1,400. How much will their escrow payment change per month?

A) Increase by $16.67
B) Increase by $20
C) Decrease by $16.67
D) No change

16. If a borrower earns $4,500 monthly and has a $1,500 mortgage payment, $300 in auto loans, and $200 in credit card payments, what is their back-end DTI ratio?

A) 22%
B) 33%
C) 44%
D) 55%

17. What is the effective monthly interest rate on a $200,000 mortgage at an annual rate of 6%?

A) 0.5%

B) 1%

C) 1.5%

D) 0.05%

18. For an initial escrow deposit, a lender requires 6 months of homeowner's insurance at $100 per month and 3 months of property taxes at $300 per month. How much must the borrower deposit into escrow at closing?

A) $600

B) $900

C) $1,200

D) $1,500

19. A $250,000 30-year fixed-rate mortgage has a 2% annual property tax rate. What is the annual property tax contribution to the PITI payment?

A) $4,000

B) $5,000

C) $6,000

D) $7,000

20. After a year, a borrower has paid $12,000 towards their mortgage, of which $8,000 was interest. What is the principal amount paid?

A) $2,000

B) $4,000

C) $6,000

D) $8,000

Correct Answes for Practice Exam 2: Real Estate Financing

1. A) 90%

- A 10% down payment on a $300,000 home leaves a loan amount of $270,000, making the LTV ratio 90%.

2. B) $12,500

- Paying 1 point reduces the interest rate, resulting in significant interest savings over 30 years, which can be calculated using an amortization formula.

3. A) $1,122.61

- The monthly principal and interest payment for a $250,000 mortgage at a 3.5% annual interest rate for 30 years can be calculated using the standard mortgage payment formula.

4. D) $1,593.54

- Adding the monthly principal and interest payment to the monthly allocations for property taxes ($4,800/12) and homeowner's insurance ($1,200/12) gives the total PITI payment.

5. B) $126

- The monthly PMI payment on a $180,000 loan with a 0.7% PMI rate is calculated as $180,000 * 0.007 / 12.

6. C) 40%

- The back-end DTI ratio is calculated by dividing total monthly debt payments ($2,000) by gross monthly income ($5,000), then multiplying by 100.

7. C) $1,000

  - Two months of property taxes ($4,800/12*2) and insurance premiums ($1,200/12*2) require an upfront escrow payment.

8. C) $250,000

  - An additional annual principal payment reduces the total interest paid, with the specific savings depending on the loan amount and interest rate.

9. B) $909.12

  - Recasting the loan with a $40,000 principal payment reduces the monthly payment, calculated with the new loan balance at the same interest rate and remaining term.

10. B) 18 months

  - Dividing the refinancing costs ($3,600) by the monthly savings ($150) gives the break-even period in months.

11. A) $1,796.18

  - The maximum possible payment occurs if the rate adjusts to the cap quickly, significantly affecting the monthly payment calculated with the adjusted interest rate.

12. A) $30,000

  - An 80% LTV on a $150,000 loan requires a $30,000 down payment to maintain that LTV ratio.

13. D) $89,528.39

  - Total interest paid can be calculated using an amortization schedule for the given loan parameters.

14. A) Increases by $25

- The yearly increase in property tax affects the monthly PITI payment proportionally to the increase divided over 12 months.

15. A) Increase by $16.67

- The increase in the annual homeowner's insurance premium affects the monthly escrow payment by the annual increase divided by 12.

16. B) 33%

- The back-end DTI ratio includes all debt payments divided by gross monthly income, calculated for the given figures.

17. A) 0.5%

- The effective monthly interest rate is the annual rate divided by 12.

18. C) $1,200

- The initial escrow deposit is the sum of six months of insurance and three months of property taxes.

19. B) $5,000

- The annual property tax contribution is calculated as 2% of the $250,000 mortgage.

20. B) $4,000

- The principal amount paid in the first year is the difference between the total payments and the interest portion.

Practice Exam 3: Real Estate Financing

Instructions:

Select the correct answer for each advanced math-focused question related to real estate financing. Ensure a deep understanding of calculations, ratios, and financial strategies within the mortgage landscape.

1. A borrower refinances a $220,000 mortgage from a 5% interest rate to a 4% interest rate for the remaining 20 years. What is the approximate monthly savings?

A) $100

B) $150

C) $200

D) $250

2. If a borrower has a monthly gross income of $6,000 and total monthly debts of $2,200, what is their front-end DTI ratio for a mortgage payment of $1,400?

A) 23.33%

B) 36.67%

C) 20%

D) 33.33%

3. For a 15-year mortgage of $300,000 at a 3% annual interest rate, what is the total amount paid towards interest over the life of the loan?

A) $45,000

B) $75,000

C) $95,000

D) $135,000

4. A homeowner pays $1,200 annually into an escrow account for homeowner's insurance. If the insurance premium increases by 10%, how much will the monthly escrow contribution increase?

A) $10

B) $12

C) $15

D) $20

5. If a $250,000 loan has a 1.2% annual PMI rate and the borrower has already paid $3,000 in PMI, how many years have they been paying PMI?

A) 1 year

B) 2 years

C) 3 years

D) 4 years

6. How much less in interest does a borrower pay on a $200,000, 30-year mortgage at 3.5% interest compared to a 4% interest rate?

A) $20,000

B) $25,000

C) $30,000

D) $35,000

7. A property assessed at $400,000 is subject to property taxes at a rate of 1.25% annually. What is the monthly tax contribution to an escrow account?

A) $416.67

B) $500

C) $625

D) $750

8. Calculating the LTV ratio for a $280,000 home purchase with a $56,000 down payment results in what percentage?

A) 75%

B) 80%

C) 85%

D) 90%

9. What is the impact on the monthly payment (principal and interest) of a $300,000 loan at 4% interest for 30 years if an additional $10,000 is paid towards the principal after one year?

A) Decreases by $30

B) Decreases by $45

C) Decreases by $50

D) Decreases by $60

10. After three years, a homeowner decides to make a lump-sum payment of $15,000 towards the principal of their $250,000, 30-year mortgage at 4%. What is the new balance?

A) $230,000

B) $235,000

C) $245,000

D) $250,000 - $15,000 minus principal paid in 3 years (calculate based on amortization).

11. A borrower with a $500,000 mortgage at 5% interest decides to switch to bi-weekly payments. How much interest can be saved over the life of the loan?

A) $10,000

B) $30,000

C) $50,000

D) $70,000

12. When a borrower's annual homeowner's insurance premium decreases from $1,500 to $1,350, how much does their monthly PITI payment decrease, assuming no other changes?

A) $12.50

B) $15

C) $20

D) $25

13. For a home valued at $350,000, what is the minimum down payment required to avoid PMI for a conventional loan?

A) $35,000

B) $50,000

C) $70,000

D) $100,000

14. If a borrower pays $2,000 annually into an escrow account for property taxes, what is the property's assessed value if the tax rate is 2%?

A) $50,000

B) $75,000

C) $100,000

D) $125,000

15. A borrower takes a $180,000 mortgage at a 4% interest rate. If they make a one-time additional payment of $5,000 towards the principal at the beginning of the second year, how much total interest will they save over the life of the loan?

A) $4,000

B) $6,000

C) $8,000

D) $10,000

16. What is the effective interest rate if a borrower takes a $300,000 loan with a 30-year term at a 3.8% nominal rate, but pays 2 points upfront?

A) 3.6%

B) 3.8%

C) 4.0%

D) 4.2%

17. How much interest does a borrower pay in the first month of a $200,000, 30-year fixed-rate mortgage at 3.5% interest?

A) $583.33

B) $600

C) $666.67

D) $700

18. A homeowner wants to lower their monthly mortgage payment by $100 by refinancing to a lower interest rate, costing $4,000 in fees. How many months will it take to recoup the refinancing costs?

A) 20 months

B) 30 months

C) 40 months

D) 50 months

19. If a borrower's property tax is $3,600 a year and their homeowner's insurance is $1,200 a year, what is their total annual contribution to the escrow account?

A) $3,000

B) $4,800

C) $5,400

D) $6,000

20. A loan of $400,000 is taken out at a 6% interest rate. If the borrower wants to reduce their interest expense by $24,000 by making a lump-sum payment, how much should the payment be?

A) $50,000

B) $60,000

C) $70,000

D) $80,000

Correct Answers For Practice Exam 3: Real Estate Financing

1. C) $200

- Refinancing to a lower interest rate reduces monthly interest costs. The exact savings can be calculated comparing the original and new amortization schedules.

2. A) 23.33%

- The front-end DTI ratio is calculated using the mortgage payment ($1,400) divided by gross monthly income ($6,000), showing the portion of income that goes toward housing.

3. B) $75,000

- The total interest paid on a 15-year mortgage can be calculated using an amortization schedule, with a 3% interest rate resulting in significant but relatively lower total interest due to the shorter term.

4. B) $12

- A 10% increase on an annual $1,200 insurance premium results in an additional $120 yearly or $10 monthly increase in the escrow contribution.

5. C) 3 years

- At a 0.7% annual PMI rate on a $180,000 loan, the PMI costs $1,260 annually. Three years of payments equal approximately $3,780, closely matching the given total PMI payment.

6. C) $30,000

- The difference in interest paid over the life of the loan between rates can be substantial, calculated using the difference in total interest from amortization schedules at 3.5% and 4%.

7. B) $500

- Annual property taxes of $5,000 (1.25% of $400,000) result in monthly contributions of $500 to the escrow account.

8. B) 80%

- A $56,000 down payment on a $280,000 purchase price results in an LTV ratio of 80%, indicating the mortgage covers 80% of the home's value.

9. B) Decreases by $45

- Applying a lump sum to the principal reduces future interest costs and slightly lowers the monthly payment due to the decreased balance.

10. B) $235,000

- Subtracting the lump-sum payment from the original balance, adjusted for principal paid, gives the new balance. This question assumes prior payments have slightly reduced the balance from $250,000.

11. C) $50,000

- Switching to bi-weekly payments accelerates the repayment schedule, reducing the interest over the life of the loan due to more frequent payments.

12. A) $12.50

- The decrease in the insurance premium reduces the monthly escrow payment proportionally, based on the annual savings divided by 12 months.

13. C) $70,000

- To avoid PMI on a conventional loan, a 20% down payment is required, which is $70,000 for a $350,000 home.

14. C) $100,000

- With a 2% tax rate, a $2,000 annual tax payment implies the property's assessed value is $100,000.

15. C) $8,000

- Making an additional payment towards the principal early in the loan term can significantly reduce the total interest paid over the life of the loan due to decreased interest accumulation.

16. D) 4.2%

- Paying points upfront effectively increases the overall cost of borrowing, which can be reflected as a higher effective interest rate when amortized over the loan term.

17. A) $583.33

- The first month's interest on a $200,000 loan at 3.5% annual interest is calculated as $200,000 * (3.5% / 12).

18. C) 40 months

- The recoup time for refinancing costs is calculated by dividing the total cost by monthly savings, showing how long it takes for the savings to offset the initial expense.

19. B) $4,800

- The total annual contribution to the escrow account for taxes ($3,600) and insurance ($1,200) combined.

20. B) $60,000

- The lump-sum payment required to achieve a specific reduction in interest expense depends on various factors, including the interest rate and remaining term. This requires detailed amortization calculations to determine exact savings.

Calculations for Real Estate Transactions

This chapter delves into the critical calculations involved in real estate transactions, providing buyers, sellers, and professionals with the mathematical tools needed to navigate the complexities of buying and selling property. Understanding these calculations is vital for making informed decisions and ensuring financial readiness.

Cost per Square Foot and Price per Acre

Understanding the cost per square foot and the price per acre is crucial in evaluating real estate investments, whether you're buying a home, a commercial property, or land. These metrics provide a basis for comparison across different properties and help investors and buyers make informed decisions.

Cost per Square Foot

The cost per square foot is a common metric used to compare the value of properties of different sizes. It's especially useful in residential and commercial real estate to gauge market trends, property values, and to budget for construction projects.

Calculation:

To determine the cost per square foot, divide the sale price or the estimated value of a property by its total interior square footage.

Cost per Square Foot = Sale Price or Property Value/Total Square Footage

Example:

If a house is sold for $300,000 and has 2,000 square feet of interior space, the cost per square foot would be:

Cost per Square Foot = 300,000/2,000 = $150

This means each square foot of the house costs $150, providing a straightforward way to compare it against other properties in the area.

Importance:

- ***Comparative Analysis:*** Enables buyers and investors to compare the value of different properties.
- ***Budgeting:*** Helps in estimating construction or renovation costs.
- ***Market Trends:*** Indicates the average prices in a specific area, useful for identifying market trends.

Price per Acre

The price per acre is predominantly used in the valuation and sale of land. It offers a standardized way to compare land parcels of varying sizes and is critical in rural, agricultural, and undeveloped land transactions.

Calculation:

The price per acre is calculated by dividing the sale price or value of the land by its area in acres.

Price per Acre = Sale Price or Land Value/Total Acres

Example:

For a parcel of land sold at $500,000 that spans 50 acres, the price per acre would be:

Price per Acre = 500,000/50 = $10,000

This calculation shows that each acre of this particular parcel costs $10,000, simplifying comparisons with other parcels.

Importance:

- **Land Evaluation:** Essential for assessing the value of land, especially in agricultural or rural investments.
- **Investment Decisions:** Assists investors in determining the potential return on investment for land development projects.

- **Zoning and Use Considerations:** Helps in evaluating land based on its potential use, zoning regulations, and development costs.

The cost per square foot and price per acre are indispensable metrics in the real estate industry, providing a foundation for valuation, comparison, and financial planning. By understanding and applying these calculations, stakeholders can navigate the complexities of real estate transactions with greater confidence and precision.

Commissions, Down Payment, and Buyer Funds

Navigating the financial intricacies of real estate transactions is crucial for both buyers and sellers. Understanding commissions, down payments, and the total funds required by buyers are essential steps in this process. These elements not only influence the immediate costs associated with purchasing a property but also affect long-term financial planning and investment strategy.

Commissions

Real estate commissions are fees paid to real estate agents for their services, typically charged as a percentage of the sale price of the property. These fees are usually split between the buyer's and seller's agents and are paid out by the seller at closing.

Calculation:
The total commission is calculated as a percentage of the property's sale price. Commonly, this rate ranges between 5% to 6% in many markets, though it can vary.

Total Commission = Sale Price x Commission Rate

For example, if a home sells for $300,000 with a commission rate of 6%, the total commission would be $18,000. This amount is then divided between the buyer's and seller's agents according to their agreement.

Impact on Transactions:

- Sellers need to account for commission fees when setting the listing price.
- Buyers indirectly affect commissions through the offer price, influencing the final sale price.

Down Payment

The down payment is the portion of the property's purchase price that the buyer pays upfront, not financed through a mortgage. It represents the buyer's initial equity in the property.

Calculation:

Down payments are typically expressed as a percentage of the purchase price. For example, a 20% down payment on a $300,000 home would be $60,000.

Down Payment = Purchase Price x Down Payment Percentage

Influence on Financing:

- A larger down payment can result in more favorable mortgage terms, including lower interest rates.
- Down payments of less than 20% often require the buyer to pay for private mortgage insurance (PMI), increasing monthly expenses.

Buyer Funds

Total Requirement:

Beyond the down payment, buyers must prepare for additional expenses, including closing costs, inspection fees, and moving expenses. The total funds required encompass all these costs plus the down payment.

Estimating Total Funds:

To accurately estimate the total funds needed, buyers must consider:

- **Down Payment:** Based on the agreed purchase price.

- **Closing Costs:** Including loan origination fees, appraisal fees, and title insurance, typically ranging from 2% to 5% of the loan amount.
- **Prepaid Expenses:** Such as property taxes, homeowners insurance, and possibly the first month's mortgage payment.

For a $300,000 home with a 20% down payment and estimated closing costs of 3%, the calculation would be:

Total Funds Needed} = Down Payment + (Purchase Price x Closing Cost Percentage)

Total Funds Needed = $60,000 + ($300,000 x 0.03) = $69,000

Understanding the dynamics of commissions, down payments, and the total funds required is fundamental for anyone involved in a real estate transaction. These components directly impact the financial responsibilities of the buyer and the net proceeds received by the seller. By carefully planning and calculating these expenses, buyers can ensure they are financially prepared for the purchase, while sellers can set realistic expectations for their net proceeds from the sale.

Seller Proceeds and Calculating Equity

When engaging in the sale of a property, understanding how to calculate seller proceeds and equity is crucial. These figures not only reflect the financial outcome of the sale for the seller but also provide insight into the financial health of the property investment over time.

Seller Proceeds

Seller proceeds represent the net amount a seller receives from the transaction after all deductions are made. This figure is pivotal in determining the financial benefit of the sale to the seller.

Calculating Seller Proceeds:

To calculate seller proceeds, subtract all associated costs of the sale from the gross sale price. These costs include the remaining mortgage balance, real estate commissions, and any other closing costs or seller-paid concessions.

Seller Proceeds = Sale Price - (Remaining Mortgage Balance + Commissions + Closing Costs)

Example:

If a property sells for $500,000, with a remaining mortgage balance of $300,000, commissions of $30,000, and closing costs of $10,000, the seller proceeds would be:

Seller Proceeds = $500,000 - ($300,000 + $30,000 + $10,000) = $160,000

Impact on the Seller:

- The proceeds provide the seller with a clear picture of the net financial gain from the sale.
- Understanding these figures helps sellers make informed decisions about pricing and negotiating sales terms.

Calculating Equity

Equity is the portion of the property's value that the owner truly "owns." It's the difference between the property's current market value and the remaining balance on any mortgages or liens against the property.

Calculation:

Equity can be calculated using the following formula:

Equity = Current Market Value - Remaining Mortgage Balance

Example:

If a homeowner's property is valued at $500,000 and they owe $300,000 on their mortgage, their equity in the home is:

Equity = $500,000 - $300,000 = $200,000

Significance of Equity:

- Equity represents the homeowner's financial stake in the property and can be a critical source of wealth and financial security.
- Increasing equity can provide opportunities for refinancing, obtaining home equity loans, or funding other investments.
- Understanding equity dynamics is essential for both short-term financial planning and long-term investment strategies.

Calculating seller proceeds and equity is fundamental in real estate transactions, offering insights into the financial returns and health of property investments. These calculations help sellers understand their net gains from a sale and gauge their investment's growth over time. For buyers and investors, understanding these concepts is equally important, as they impact decisions related to property acquisition, financing, and long-term property management. By mastering these financial calculations, stakeholders can make informed decisions, ensuring successful and profitable real estate endeavors.

Property Taxes, Transfer Tax, and Housing Expenses

In real estate, managing and understanding ongoing and transactional costs is crucial for both buyers and sellers. Among these, property taxes, transfer taxes, and various housing expenses play significant roles in the financial dynamics of owning, buying, or selling property.

Property Taxes

Property taxes are recurring annual charges levied by local governments on real estate. These taxes fund public services such as schools, roads, and emergency services. The amount owed is typically based on the assessed value of the property and the tax rate set by the local jurisdiction.

Calculation:
The formula for calculating property taxes is:

Property Taxes = Assessed Value x Tax Rate

Example:
If a home is assessed at $300,000 and the local tax rate is 1.5%, the annual property taxes would be:

$300,000 x 0.015 = $4,500

Implications for Owners:
- Property taxes can significantly affect the overall cost of homeownership.
- Fluctuations in property value or tax rates can lead to changes in annual tax liabilities.

Transfer Tax

Transfer tax is imposed by a state or local government on the transfer of property from one owner to another. It's usually calculated based on the sale price of the property.

Calculation:
The formula depends on the specific rate set by the jurisdiction, often a percentage of the sale price:

Transfer Tax = Sale Price x Transfer Tax Rate

Example:

For a property sale price of $500,000 in an area with a transfer tax rate of 1%:

$500,000 x 0.01 = $5,000

Role in Transactions:

- Transfer taxes can vary widely by location.
- They are typically paid by the seller, but negotiation may shift this responsibility to the buyer.

Housing Expenses

Scope:

Beyond mortgage payments, homeowners incur various ongoing expenses related to the maintenance and operation of their property. These include:

- *Homeowners Insurance:* Protects against loss or damage.
- *Maintenance and Repairs:* Regular upkeep costs to maintain property value and functionality.
- *Utilities:* Water, electricity, gas, and internet services.
- *Homeowners Association (HOA) Fees:* Applicable in certain communities for amenities and services.

Managing Expenses:

Understanding and budgeting for these expenses are crucial aspects of responsible homeownership. They can vary based on property size, location, and individual usage patterns.

Example:

Annual homeowners insurance might cost $1,200, maintenance $2,000, utilities $3,600, and HOA fees $2,400, totaling:

$1,200 + $2,000 + $3,600 + $2,400 = $9,200

Property taxes, transfer taxes, and housing expenses are integral parts of the financial landscape in real estate. Effectively managing and understanding these costs is essential for both current homeowners planning their budgets and potential buyers assessing the affordability of a property. For sellers, these expenses can influence the net proceeds from a sale, while buyers need to consider them when calculating the total cost of acquiring and maintaining a home.

Closing Costs and Allocating Expenses - Proration

When finalizing a real estate transaction, understanding closing costs and the concept of proration is vital. These elements play a crucial role in determining the final financial obligations of both the buyer and seller.

Closing Costs

Closing costs encompass the various fees, taxes, and other expenses that are paid at the closing of a real estate transaction. These costs are over and above the price of the property itself and can be incurred by either the buyer, the seller, or both, depending on the terms of the sale and local regulations.

Components:
Closing costs can include, but are not limited to:
- *Loan Origination Fees:* Charged by the lender for processing the new loan.
- *Appraisal Fees:* Paid to assess the property's fair market value.
- *Title Search and Insurance:* Ensures the property is free of liens and establishes insurance to protect against future claims.
- *Attorney Fees:* For legal services related to the transaction.
- *Recording Fees:* Charged by the local government to record the sale and loan transaction.
- *Transfer Taxes:* Taxes imposed on the transfer of property title.

Calculation:

While the exact amount can vary, closing costs typically range between 2% to 5% of the purchase price of the property. For example, on a $300,000 home, closing costs can be between $6,000 and $15,000.

Closing Costs = Purchase Price x Closing Costs Percentage

Implications:

Buyers should budget for these costs in addition to their down payment, while sellers may agree to cover certain expenses to finalize the sale.

Allocating Expenses - Proration

Proration is the process of dividing financial responsibilities between the buyer and seller based on the exact time each party is in possession of the property. Common prorated items include property taxes, homeowners association (HOA) fees, and utilities.

Methodology:

Proration is typically calculated by determining the daily cost of an expense, then multiplying that by the number of days the seller owned the property during the billing period.

$$\textbf{Daily Cost} = \frac{Annual\ Cost}{365}$$

Prorated Amount = Daily Cost x Days Owned

Example:

If a seller has paid annual property taxes of $3,650 but sells the home halfway through the year, the prorated amount owed back to the seller would be:

$$\text{Daily Cost} = \frac{3650}{365} = \$\ 10$$

Prorated Amount for Half Year = $10 x 182.5 = $1,825

Significance:

- *Fair Allocation:* Proration ensures that both buyers and sellers only pay for their portion of shared expenses.

- *Closing Adjustments:* These calculations are made at closing, adjusting the final amounts owed by each party.

Closing costs and the proration of expenses are critical components of the financial transactions involved in buying or selling property. They require careful consideration and accurate calculation to ensure both parties fulfill their financial obligations appropriately. Understanding these aspects allows buyers to adequately prepare for the total cost of their purchase and sellers to accurately anticipate their net proceeds from the sale. Effective negotiation and clear communication between all parties, often facilitated by real estate professionals, can help manage these costs and ensure a smooth transaction.

Practice Exam 1: Calculations for Real Estate Transactions

Instructions:

Choose the correct answer for each question. This exam covers essential calculations involved in real estate transactions, including metrics for property valuation, financial obligations of buyers and sellers, and more.

1. How is the cost per square foot of a property calculated?

A) Divide the property's acreage by its sale price.

B) Divide the sale price by the total square footage.

C) Multiply the square footage by the property taxes.

D) Multiply the sale price by the number of rooms.

2. If a 50-acre land parcel sells for $500,000, what is the price per acre?

A) $5,000

B) $10,000

C) $25,000

D) $50,000

3. What percentage of the sale price is typically paid in commissions to real estate agents?

A) 1-2%

B) 3-4%

C) 5-6%

D) 7-8%

4. A buyer pays a down payment of 20% on a $250,000 home. How much is the down payment?

A) $25,000

B) $40,000

C) $50,000

D) $60,000

5. Seller proceeds are calculated by subtracting what from the sale price?

A) The original purchase price of the home

B) The mortgage balance, commissions, and closing costs

C) The buyer's down payment

D) The annual property tax

6. Equity in a home is defined as the difference between:

A) The sale price and the original purchase price.

B) The current market value and the remaining mortgage balance.

C) The down payment and the loan amount.

D) The mortgage balance and the annual interest paid.

7. Annual property taxes on a home valued at $400,000 are $8,000. What is the tax rate?

A) 0.5%

B) 1%

C) 2%

D) 2.5%

8. Transfer taxes are usually calculated based on:

A) The home's assessed value.

B) The sale price of the property.

C) The mortgage amount.

D) The down payment amount.

9. Which of the following is not a typical housing expense?

A) Utilities

B) Homeowner's association fees

C) Property insurance

D) Transfer tax

10. Closing costs for a buyer are typically what percentage of the home purchase price?

A) 1-2%

B) 2-5%

C) 5-7%

D) 7-10%

11. Proration at closing might be necessary for which of the following expenses?

A) Buyer's down payment

B) Seller's moving costs

C) Property taxes

D) Real estate agent commissions

12. If a homeowner's insurance premium is $1,200 per year, what is the monthly cost included in the PITI payment?

A) $100

B) $200

C) $300

D) $400

13. A property is rented for $2,000 per month. What is the annual rental income?

A) $12,000

B) $18,000

C) $24,000

D) $30,000

14. How much are the annual insurance premiums if the monthly cost included in the PITI is $150?

A) $1,200

B) $1,500

C) $1,800

D) $2,000

15. What is the first step in calculating seller proceeds?

A) Determining the sale price

B) Subtracting the down payment

C) Adding the property taxes

D) Calculating the commission

16. If a seller needs to pay 2 months of property tax for proration at closing, and the annual tax is $4,800, how much is due?

A) $400
B) $800
C) $1,200
D) $2,400

17. Closing costs paid by the buyer are $6,000 on a $200,000 purchase. What percentage of the purchase price are the closing costs?

A) 2%
B) 3%
C) 4%
D) 5%

18. A buyer negotiates a 5% commission rate with their real estate agent on a $300,000 home purchase. How much will the commission be?

A) $5,000
B) $10,000
C) $15,000
D) $20,000

19. If a 100-acre farm sells for $1,000,000, what is the cost per acre?

A) $1,000
B) $5,000
C) $10,000
D) $100,000

20. The transfer tax rate in a certain jurisdiction is 1% of the sale price. For a property sold at $500,000, how much is the transfer tax?

A) $500

B) $1,000

C) $5,000

D) $10,000

Correct Answers for Practice Exam 1 : Calculations for Real Estate Transactions

1. B) Divide the sale price by the total square footage.

- Correct because the cost per square foot is determined by dividing the total cost of the property by its square footage, providing a standard measure for comparing property values.

2. B) $10,000

- The price per acre is found by dividing the total sale price by the number of acres. $500,000 / 50 acres = $10,000 per acre, allowing for comparison across different land sizes.

3. C) 5-6%

- This is the typical range for real estate commissions, which are calculated as a percentage of the property's sale price.

4. C) $50,000

- A 20% down payment on a $250,000 home is calculated as 0.20 * $250,000 = $50,000, representing the buyer's initial equity.

5. B) The mortgage balance, commissions, and closing costs

- Seller proceeds are calculated by subtracting these expenses from the sale price to determine the net amount received by the seller.

6. B) The current market value and the remaining mortgage balance.

- Equity is the difference between the property's current market value and what is still owed on the mortgage, reflecting the owner's financial stake in the property.

7. B) 2%

- If annual property taxes are $8,000 on a home valued at $400,000, the tax rate is calculated as ($8,000 / $400,000) * 100 = 2%.

8. B) The sale price of the property.

- Transfer taxes are calculated based on the sale price, typically as a percentage, varying by jurisdiction.

9. D) Transfer tax

- Transfer tax is a one-time expense paid during the transfer of property ownership, not a recurring housing expense like the others listed.

10. B) 2-5%

- Closing costs, which include various fees and expenses related to finalizing a real estate transaction, typically range from 2% to 5% of the purchase price.

11. C) Property taxes

- Property taxes are often prorated at closing, meaning the seller credits the buyer for taxes paid for the portion of the year the seller won't own the property.

12. A) $100

- The annual homeowner's insurance premium divided by 12 months gives the monthly cost included in PITI, ensuring the property is insured.

13. C) $24,000

- The annual rental income from a property rented at $2,000 per month is calculated as $2,000 * 12 = $24,000, indicating the property's income-generating potential.

14. C) $1,800

- If the monthly insurance cost included in the PITI payment is $150, the annual cost is $150 * 12 = $1,800, reflecting the yearly insurance expense.

15. A) Determining the sale price

- The first step in calculating seller proceeds is to know the sale price, from which all deductions (like mortgage balance, commissions, and closing costs) will be subtracted.

16. B) $800

- Two months of property taxes on an annual bill of $4,800 are calculated as ($4,800 / 12) * 2 = $800, representing the seller's portion of the tax year.

17. B) 3%

- The closing costs of $6,000 on a $200,000 purchase represent 3% of the purchase price ($6,000 / $200,000 = 0.03 or 3%).

18. C) $15,000

- A 5% commission on a $300,000 sale is $300,000 * 0.05 = $15,000, paid to the real estate agents involved in the transaction.

19. C) $10,000

- For a 100-acre farm sold at $1,000,000, the cost per acre is $1,000,000 / 100 = $10,000, helping to compare value across different land parcels.

20. C) $5,000

- A 1% transfer tax on a $500,000 sale is $500,000 * 0.01 = $5,000, indicating the government levy for transferring property ownership.

Practice Exam 2: Calculations for Real Estate Transactions

Instructions:

Select the correct answer for each advanced question related to the calculations involved in real estate transactions. This exam tests depth of understanding in property valuation, financial obligations, and proration techniques.

1. What is the monthly property tax payment for a house valued at $360,000 with an annual tax rate of 1.25%?

A) $300

B) $375

C) $450

D) $500

2. If a buyer secures a mortgage for $280,000 and the lender requires a 1.5% origination fee, how much will the fee be?

A) $2,800

B) $3,200

C) $4,200

D) $4,500

3. For a commercial property sold at $2 million with a commission rate of 3%, what total commission is paid to the brokerage?

A) $30,000

B) $60,000

C) $90,000

D) $120,000

4. A homebuyer plans to make a 15% down payment on a home listed at $400,000. How much is the down payment?

A) $40,000

B) $50,000

C) $60,000

D) $80,000

5. If closing costs are estimated to be 3% of the home's purchase price of $250,000, how much are the closing costs?

A) $5,000

B) $7,500

C) $10,000

D) $12,500

6. How much equity does a homeowner have in a property valued at $500,000 with a remaining mortgage balance of $300,000?

A) $100,000

B) $200,000

C) $300,000

D) $400,000

7. A property's assessed value increases from $250,000 to $260,000. If the tax rate is 1.2%, how much does the annual property tax increase by?

A) $100

B) $120

C) $200

D) $120

8. Transfer tax on a $600,000 sale is $9,000. What is the transfer tax rate?

A) 0.5%

B) 1.0%

C) 1.5%

D) 2.0%

9. What is the prorated amount for a utility bill of $600 for a month, if closing is set for 15 days into the billing cycle?

A) $200

B) $300

C) $400

D) $500

10. If a homeowner's insurance premium is $2,400 annually, what is the prorated monthly cost for a buyer closing on the home halfway through the insurance policy term?

A) $100

B) $200

C) $1,200

D) $2,400

11. A rental property generates $24,000 annually. What is the monthly rental income?

A) $1,000

B) $2,000

C) $3,000

D) $4,000

12. A seller agrees to cover $5,000 of the buyer's closing costs on a $300,000 sale. What percentage of the sale price does this represent?

A) 1.67%

B) 2.5%

C) 1.5%

D) 3%

13. If a property sells for $450,000 and the buyer pays 2% in closing costs, how much are the buyer's closing costs?

A) $6,000

B) $8,000

C) $9,000

D) $10,000

14. A seller pays a transfer tax of $4,500 on the sale of their property. If the transfer tax rate is 1.5%, what was the sale price?

A) $200,000

B) $300,000

C) $400,000

D) $500,000

15. For a property valued at $350,000 with a 20% down payment, what is the loan amount?

A) $70,000

B) $280,000

C) $300,000

D) $350,000

16. A buyer negotiates to pay 75% of the total $8,000 property tax bill for the year. How much will the buyer pay?

A) $2,000

B) $4,000

C) $6,000

D) $8,000

17. Closing on a property is scheduled for June 15. The seller has prepaid the property taxes for the year at $4,800. How much of the property tax is the buyer responsible for, assuming 360 days for calculation?

A) $2,400

B) $2,600

C) $2,800

D) $3,000

18. If a home with an annual insurance premium of $1,500 sells, and closing is on July 1, how much is the buyer's prorated insurance responsibility for the year?

A) $750

B) $1,500

C) $1,250

D) $1,000

19. A property is rented for $1,800 a month. If the landlord increases the rent by 5%, what will be the new monthly rent?

A) $1,890

B) $1,900

C) $1,950

D) $2,000

20. A real estate transaction includes a transfer tax of 1% of the sale price. If the transfer tax paid is $3,750, what was the sale price of the property?

A) $375,000

B) $350,000

C) $400,000

D) $300,000

Correct Answers for Practice Exam 2 : Calculations for Real Estate Transactions

1. B) $375

 - Annual property tax is calculated as $360,000 * 1.25% = $4,500. Monthly payment: $4,500 / 12 = $375.

2. C) $4,200

 - Loan origination fee: $280,000 * 1.5% = $4,200.

3. B) $60,000

 - Commission: $2,000,000 * 3% = $60,000.

4. C) $60,000

 - Down payment: $400,000 * 15% = $60,000.

5. B) $7,500

 - Closing costs: $250,000 * 3% = $7,500.

6. B) $200,000

 - Equity: $500,000 (current value) - $300,000 (mortgage balance) = $200,000.

7. B) $120

 - Tax increase: ($260,000 - $250,000) * 1.2% = $120.

8. C) 1.5%

 - Transfer tax rate calculation: $9,000 / $600,000 = 1.5%.

9. B) $300

- Prorated utility bill for 15 days: $600 / 30 days * 15 days = $300.

10. A) $100

- Half of the annual premium: $2,400 / 12 months = $200; for half the year = $1,200 (since the policy term is halfway, the monthly cost remains as originally divided).

11. B) $2,000

- Monthly rental income: $24,000 / 12 months = $2,000.

12. A) 1.67%

- Seller covering $5,000 of buyer's closing costs: $5,000 / $300,000 = 1.67%.

13. C) $9,000

- Buyer's closing costs: $450,000 * 2% = $9,000.

14. B) $300,000

- Sale price from transfer tax: $4,500 / 1.5% = $300,000.

15. B) $280,000

- Loan amount after down payment: $350,000 - ($350,000 * 20%) = $280,000.

16. C) $6,000

- Buyer pays 75% of property tax: $8,000 * 75% = $6,000.

17. B) $2,600

- Assuming a 360-day year for simplicity, and with 197 days left in the year (from June 15 to December 31), the buyer's responsibility: $4,800 / 360 days * 197 days ≈ $2,600.

18. A) $750

- Prorated insurance for half the year (July 1 to December 31): $1,500 / 2 = $750.

19. A) $1,890

- New monthly rent after a 5% increase: $1,800 + ($1,800 * 5%) = $1,890.

20. A) $375,000

- Sale price from transfer tax: $3,750 / 1% = $375,000.

Practice Exam 3 : Real Estate Transaction Calculations

Instructions:

Choose the most appropriate answer for each question. This exam is designed to test a comprehensive mastery of calculations related to real estate transactions, focusing on deeper insights and more complex scenarios.

1. A house is listed at $350,000. If it sells for 95% of the listed price, what is the sale price?

A) $332,500

B) $335,000

C) $337,500

D) $340,000

2. If a property's assessed value is $280,000 and the homeowner pays $5,600 in property taxes, what is the effective property tax rate?

A) 1%

B) 2%

C) 3%

D) 4%

3. For a transaction with $8,000 in closing costs and a 1% transfer tax, what is the total amount paid in transaction-specific costs for a property sold at $400,000?

A) $4,000

B) $8,000

C) $12,000

D) $16,000

4. A buyer plans to make a 25% down payment on a property priced at $480,000. What is the amount of the down payment?

A) $100,000

B) $120,000

C) $150,000

D) $200,000

5. How much in commissions is paid on the sale of a property for $600,000 at a rate of 4%?

A) $20,000

B) $24,000

C) $28,000

D) $32,000

6. A seller has $50,000 in equity before selling their home for $300,000. If the seller pays $18,000 in commissions and $12,000 in closing costs, what is their equity after the sale?

A) $20,000

B) $270,000

C) $320,000

D) $370,000

7. If a homeowner's annual insurance premium is $1,800 and they sell the house after 9 months, how much of the insurance premium should be prorated to the buyer?

A) $450
B) $1,350
C) $1,800
D) $2,250

8. What is the new loan amount after a borrower makes a $40,000 extra payment towards the principal on their $200,000 mortgage?

A) $160,000
B) $190,000
C) $200,000
D) $240,000

9. A rental property with a monthly income of $2,500 incurs annual expenses of $12,000. What is the net annual income?

A) $18,000
B) $30,000
C) $12,000
D) $15,000

10. Closing is on April 15th, and the seller has prepaid property taxes for the year amounting to $3,600. How much should be credited to the buyer for property taxes? (Assume a 360-day year for simplicity, and that taxes are paid in advance.)

A) $900

B) $1,800

C) $2,700

D) $3,600

11. A buyer is purchasing a lot for $75,000 and pays a 2% origination fee. How much is the fee?

A) $1,000

B) $1,500

C) $2,000

D) $2,500

12. If a homeowner refinances their mortgage and the closing costs are $6,000, which are 3% of the new mortgage amount, what is the new mortgage amount?

A) $180,000

B) $200,000

C) $220,000

D) $240,000

13. A commercial property is sold with a 2.5% commission rate on the final sale price of $800,000. What is the total commission?

A) $16,000

B) $20,000

C) $24,000

D) $30,000

14. A property assessed at $300,000 pays an annual property tax of $9,000. The owner sells the property after owning it for 240 days in the tax year. How much of the tax is the seller responsible for?

A) $6,000

B) $7,200

C) $7,500

D) $9,000

15. If a property's price per square foot is $150 and the total square footage is 2,000 sq ft, what is the total sale price?

A) $200,000

B) $250,000

C) $300,000

D) $350,000

16. The transfer tax for a property sale is $2,500 on a property that sold for $500,000. What is the transfer tax rate?

A) 0.25%

B) 0.5%

C) 0.75%

D) 1%

17. A home sells for $400,000 with annual property taxes of $6,000. What percentage of the sale price do the property taxes represent?

A) 1.25%

B) 1.5%

C) 1.75%

D) 2%

18. How much does a buyer need to pay upfront if the down payment is 10% of a $250,000 home and closing costs are $7,500?

A) $17,500

B) $25,000

C) $30,000

D) $32,500

19. If a seller pays $10,000 towards the buyer's closing costs on a $200,000 sale, what percentage of the sale price does this represent?

A) 2%

B) 4%

C) 5%

D) 10%

20. For a property with a monthly rental fee of $1,200, what is the total income generated over a year?

A) $12,000

B) $14,400

C) $24,000

D) $28,800

Correct Answers for Practice Exam 3 : Calculations for Real Estate Transactions

1. A) $332,500

  - 95% of the listed price ($350,000) calculates the sale price after applying the discount.

2. B) 2%

  - The property tax rate is found by dividing the tax amount ($5,600) by the property's assessed value ($280,000).

3. C) $12,000

  - Sum of closing costs ($8,000) and transfer tax (1% of $400,000 = $4,000**).**

4. B) $120,000

  - 25% of the property price ($480,000) gives the down payment amount.

5. B) $24,000

  - 4% commission rate applied to a $600,000 sale price.

6. B) $270,000

  - Original equity ($50,000) plus sale proceeds after subtracting commissions and closing costs from the sale price.

7. B) $1,350

  - For the 3 remaining months, the buyer is responsible for the prorated portion of the annual premium ($1,800).

8. A) $160,000

  - Subtracting the extra payment ($40,000) from the original loan amount ($200,000).

9. B) $30,000

- Annual rental income minus expenses ($2,500 * 12 - $12,000).

10. B) $1,800

- Half the annual property tax, assuming the buyer and seller split the year equally.

11. B) $1,500

- 2% of the purchase price ($75,000).

12. B) $200,000

- The new mortgage amount where $6,000 closing costs represent 3%.

13. B) $20,000

- 2.5% commission on an $800,000 sale price.

14. B) $7,200

- Property tax proportionate to the days the seller owned the property in the tax year.

15. C) $300,000

- Total sale price calculated from the cost per square foot multiplied by the total square footage.

16. B) 0.5%

- Transfer tax rate calculated from the tax amount ($2,500) relative to the sale price ($500,000).

17. B) 1.5%

- Property tax percentage of the sale price calculated from annual taxes ($6,000) relative to the sale price ($400,000).

18. D) $32,500

- Total of the down payment and closing costs.

19. C) 5%

- Percentage of the sale price represented by the seller's contribution to the buyer's closing costs.

20. C) $14,400

- Total annual income from the property calculated by multiplying the monthly rent by 12.

Investment and Profitability Analysis

Investing in real estate is a strategic endeavor that requires a thorough understanding of financial metrics to assess profitability and make informed decisions. This chapter delves into crucial calculations and concepts that underpin real estate investment analysis.

Profit/Loss and Percentage Change in Value

Understanding how to calculate profit or loss and the percentage change in a property's value is essential for real estate investors. These metrics provide insights into the financial performance of an investment, indicating its profitability and how its value has changed over time.

Profit/Loss Calculation

Profit or loss from a real estate investment is determined by comparing the total costs of acquiring and maintaining the property against the sale price or current market value if the property hasn't been sold.

Formula:

Profit/Loss = Sale Price (or Current Market Value) - Total Costs

Total Costs include:
- Purchase price
- Renovation and repair costs
- Holding costs (insurance, property taxes, maintenance)
- Selling costs (agent commissions, marketing)

Example:
An investor buys a property for $200,000, spends $50,000 on renovations, and incurs $10,000 in holding costs. If the property sells for $300,000, with $15,000 in selling costs:

Profit = $300,000 - ($200,000 + $50,000 + $10,000 + $15,000) = $25,000

This calculation shows a net profit of $25,000 from the investment.

Percentage Change in Value

The percentage change in a property's value over time reflects its appreciation or depreciation, key indicators of investment performance and market trends.

Formula:

$$\textbf{Percentage Change} = \frac{Current\ Value - Original\ Purchase\ Price}{Original\ Purchase\ Price} \textbf{ x 100\%}$$

Example:

If the original purchase price of the property was $200,000 and its current market value is $300,000:

$$\textbf{Percentage Change} = \frac{300,000 - 200,000}{200,000} \textbf{ x 100\% = 50\%}$$

This indicates a 50% increase in the property's value, demonstrating significant appreciation.

Analyzing Profit/Loss and Value Change

- *Profit/Loss Analysis:* Provides a direct measure of financial success, indicating whether an investment has generated a return. Positive profit signifies a successful investment, while a loss suggests that the investment's costs exceeded the returns.

- *Value Change:* Offers a broader perspective on how the property's market value has shifted, independent of the actual realized profit or loss. It's particularly useful for long-term investments where the property might not be immediately sold.

- *Strategic Implications:* Investors use these metrics to assess the effectiveness of their investment strategies, adjust their portfolio, and make informed decisions about future investments based on historical performance and market conditions.

Profit/loss calculations and analyzing the percentage change in property value are fundamental to real estate investment analysis. They allow investors to gauge the financial health of their investments, understand market dynamics, and plan future actions to maximize returns. Effective use of these metrics can lead to more informed investment decisions, better financial outcomes, and a stronger investment portfolio.

Depreciation in Real Estate Investments

Depreciation is a key concept in real estate investment, particularly for rental properties. It allows investors to account for the wear and tear on a property over time, offering tax benefits that can significantly impact the investment's profitability.

Depreciation is the process of expensing the cost of a tangible asset over its useful life. In real estate, it refers to the decline in the value of a building and its improvements (excluding land) due to aging, wear and tear, and technological obsolescence.

The primary purpose of depreciation is to match the cost of using a building with the income it generates each year, providing a more accurate financial picture of the investment's performance.

Determining Rental Property Depreciation

Rental properties are depreciated over a predefined period set by the IRS, which is currently 27.5 years for residential properties. This period reflects the expected "useful life" of the building.

Formula:

Annual Depreciation Expense $= \dfrac{Property\ Cost - Land\ Value}{Useful\ Life\ (27.5\ years)}$

- *Property Cost:* The purchase price of the property, including any improvements or renovations that extend its useful life.
- *Land Value:* Since land does not wear out or become obsolete, its cost is not depreciable.

Example:

If an investor purchases a rental property for $275,000, with the land valued at $75,000, the depreciable base is $200,000 ($275,000 - $75,000). The annual depreciation expense would be:

$$\text{Annual Depreciation Expense} = \frac{\$200,000}{27.5} = \$7,272.73$$

Straight-Line Method

The straight-line method is the most common approach to calculating depreciation for real estate. It assumes the property will lose an equal amount of value each year over its useful life.

- *Advantages:* Simplicity and predictability, making it easy for investors to plan for tax implications.
- *Calculation:* The formula provided above exemplifies the straight-line method.

Depreciation Recapture

Upon the sale of a depreciated property, the IRS requires investors to "recapture" the depreciation, taxing it as ordinary income up to the maximum limit. This recapture tax can impact the net proceeds from the sale.

Importance in Investment Analysis

- *Tax Deductions:* Depreciation is a non-cash deduction that reduces taxable income, effectively lowering the investor's tax liability and improving cash flow.
- *Investment Strategy:* Understanding and leveraging depreciation can enhance the overall return on investment by maximizing tax benefits.
- *Financial Planning:* Proper accounting for depreciation helps investors maintain accurate records, crucial for long-term financial planning and strategy.

Depreciation is a critical element in the financial analysis of rental properties, offering significant tax advantages that can improve the investment's bottom line. By systematically accounting for a property's depreciation, investors can gain a clearer understanding of its true earning potential, make more informed decisions, and optimize their investment strategy for better returns. Recognizing the importance of depreciation and its implications on tax and investment strategy is essential for any real estate investor aiming to maximize profitability.

Rate of Return in Real Estate Investments

The Rate of Return (RoR) is a crucial metric for evaluating the performance of real estate investments. It measures the efficiency and profitability of an investment by comparing the gains (or losses) to the initial capital outlay. Understanding and calculating the RoR helps investors make informed decisions, compare investment opportunities, and assess the financial health of their real estate portfolio.

The Rate of Return is the percentage that represents the net gain or loss of an investment over a specified period, relative to the initial investment cost. In real estate, it considers both the income generated from the property (like rent) and the appreciation (or depreciation) in the property's value.

Importance:

- ***Performance Measurement:*** RoR provides a standardized way to gauge investment performance, making it easier to compare different real estate opportunities.
- ***Investment Decisions:*** Investors use RoR to identify which properties offer the best potential returns, adjusting their strategies accordingly.
- ***Financial Planning:*** Understanding the RoR helps investors set realistic expectations and plan for future investments or expenses.

Calculating Rate of Return

The basic formula for the Rate of Return is:

$$\text{RoR} = \frac{Current\ Value\ of\ Investment - Cost\ of\ Investment}{Cost\ of\ Investment} \times 100\%$$

Components:

- *Current Value of Investment:* This includes the current market value of the property plus any income it has generated.

- *Cost of Investment:* The initial purchase price and any additional expenses incurred to make the property rentable or saleable.

Example:

If an investor purchases a property for $200,000 (cost of investment) and, after one year, the property is worth $220,000 (current value) and has generated $12,000 in rental income:

Current Value of Investment = $220,000 (market value) + $12,000 (rent) = $232,000

$$\text{RoR} = \frac{\$232,000 - \$200,000}{200,000} \times 100\% = 16\%$$

This calculation shows a 16% Rate of Return, indicating a profitable investment.

Adjusted Rate of Return

For a more accurate assessment, the Adjusted Rate of Return can be calculated by considering expenses such as maintenance costs, property taxes, insurance, and mortgage interest. This adjusted figure provides a clearer picture of the investment's true profitability after accounting for its ongoing operational costs.

Rate of Return vs. Other Metrics

While the RoR is an invaluable tool for assessing investment performance, it's often used alongside other metrics such as the Capitalization Rate (Cap Rate) and Cash on Cash Return. Each metric offers unique insights, with the RoR providing a comprehensive view that includes both income and appreciation.

The Rate of Return is a fundamental metric in real estate investment analysis, offering insights into an investment's profitability and efficiency. Accurate calculation and interpretation of the RoR enable investors to make informed decisions, optimize their investment strategies, and achieve their financial goals. As with any financial metric, considering the RoR within the broader context of market conditions, investment objectives, and risk tolerance is essential for a well-rounded investment strategy.

Gross Rent Multiplier (GRM) and Capitalization Rate (Cap Rate)

In the realm of real estate investment analysis, the Gross Rent Multiplier (GRM) and the Capitalization Rate (Cap Rate) are pivotal metrics used to evaluate the potential profitability and value of income-producing properties. Understanding these concepts allows investors to make informed decisions by assessing the income generation and return on investment of properties.

Gross Rent Multiplier (GRM)

The GRM is a real estate valuation metric that provides a simple way to compare and assess the value of income-producing properties. It is calculated by dividing the property's sale price by its annual rental income.

$$GRM = \frac{Sale\ Price}{Annual\ Gross\ Rent}$$

Application:
- *Property Comparison:* GRM is particularly useful for quickly comparing the value of similar properties in the same market.
- *Investment Screening:* A lower GRM can indicate a potentially undervalued property or a higher rental income relative to the sale price.

Example:
If a property is sold for $300,000 and generates an annual gross rent of $30,000, the GRM would be:

$$GRM = \frac{\$300,000}{\$30,000} = 10$$

A GRM of 10 means it would take 10 years for the property to pay for itself in gross rent received, excluding operating expenses.

Capitalization Rate (Cap Rate)

The Cap Rate measures the return on investment for an income-producing property, expressed as a percentage. It is calculated by dividing the Net Operating Income (NOI) by the current market value or purchase price of the property.

Formula:

$$\textbf{Cap Rate} = \frac{Net\ Operating\ Income}{Current\ Market\ Value\ or\ Purchase\ Price} \textbf{ x 100\%}$$

Application:
- *Return Evaluation:* Cap Rate helps investors evaluate the return on an investment property independent of financing.
- *Market Comparison:* It allows for comparison across different markets and property types.

Example:
If an investment property generates $40,000 in NOI and has a current market value of $500,000, the Cap Rate would be:

$$\textbf{Cap Rate} = \frac{\$40,000}{\$500,000} \textbf{ x 100\%} = \textbf{8\%}$$

An 8% Cap Rate indicates the rate of return on the property based on its current income and value, suggesting how quickly the investment would pay off under current conditions.

GRM vs. Cap Rate

- *Simplicity vs. Depth:* GRM offers a quick, easy comparison but does not account for operating expenses. Cap Rate provides a deeper analysis by considering the net income after expenses.
- *Usage:* GRM is often used for initial screenings, while Cap Rate is critical for a detailed investment analysis.
- *Preference:* The choice between GRM and Cap Rate depends on the investor's goals, the property type, and the available data.

Both GRM and Cap Rate are essential tools in the arsenal of a real estate investor. GRM provides a quick snapshot for comparing property values, while Cap Rate offers a more detailed analysis of return on investment, taking into account the operating efficiency of the property. Understanding and utilizing these metrics effectively can significantly enhance investment decision-making, allowing investors to identify profitable opportunities and optimize their investment strategies for long-term success.

Vacancy Rate in Real Estate Investment

The Vacancy Rate is a critical metric within real estate investment, offering insight into the performance and profitability of rental properties. It quantifies the portion of a property's units that are unoccupied over a specific period, typically expressed as a percentage. Understanding and managing the Vacancy Rate is essential for maintaining a healthy cash flow and maximizing the return on investment (ROI) in real estate.

Vacancy Rate measures the proportion of all available units in a rental property that remain vacant or unrented at a given time. It's a key indicator of rental demand, property management effectiveness, and market conditions.

Formula:

$$\text{Vacancy Rate} = \left(\frac{Number\ of\ Vacant\ Units}{Total\ Units\ Available} \right) \times 100\%$$

Application:

- *Performance Indicator:* A high Vacancy Rate may indicate overpricing, poor property condition, ineffective marketing, or unfavorable market conditions. Conversely, a low Vacancy Rate suggests strong demand and effective property management.

- *Financial Planning:* Investors use the Vacancy Rate to forecast income, budget for operating expenses, and evaluate the financial health of their investment properties.

Calculating Vacancy Rate

To calculate the Vacancy Rate, you need to know the total number of units available for rent and the number of those units that are currently vacant.

Example:

If a rental property has 100 units and 5 of those units are vacant:

$$\textbf{Vacancy Rate} = \left(\frac{5}{100}\right) \textbf{ x 100\%} = \textbf{5\%}$$

This calculation shows that 5% of the property's units are unoccupied, providing a quantifiable measure of vacancy levels.

Impact of Vacancy Rate on Profitability

- *Income Reduction:* Each vacant unit represents potential rental income that is not being realized, directly affecting the property's profitability.

- *Operating Costs:* Vacant units still incur costs (maintenance, utilities, marketing for tenants), which can erode the net operating income.

- *Investment Valuation:* Higher vacancy rates can lower the property's valuation due to the anticipated lower income streams.

Strategies to Minimize Vacancy Rate

1. Competitive Pricing: Ensure rental rates are competitive within the local market to attract tenants.

2. Property Upkeep: Maintain the property in good condition to make it more appealing to potential renters.

3. Effective Marketing: Use various marketing channels to reach potential tenants, including online listings, social media, and local advertising.

4. Tenant Retention: Implement strategies to retain tenants, such as offering renewal incentives, promptly addressing maintenance issues, and fostering good landlord-tenant relationships.

The Vacancy Rate is a vital metric in real estate investment, reflecting the property's marketability and operational efficiency. A low Vacancy Rate indicates strong demand and effective management, contributing to the investment's success. Conversely, a high Vacancy Rate signals potential issues that need addressing. By actively managing and strategizing to reduce vacancies, investors can enhance their property's income potential and overall investment returns, ensuring long-term profitability and success in the competitive real estate market.

Practice Exam 1: Investment and Profitability Analysis in Real Estate

Instructions:

Select the correct answer for each question related to the topics of investment and profitability analysis in real estate. This exam covers essential concepts including profit/loss calculations, depreciation, rate of return, gross rent multiplier (GRM), capitalization rate (Cap Rate), and vacancy rate.

1. How do you calculate the profit or loss on a real estate investment?

A) Sale Price - Purchase Price

B) Sale Price - (Purchase Price + Expenses)

C) (Sale Price + Rental Income) - Purchase Price

D) Sale Price + Depreciation

2. What represents a 10% increase in the value of a property originally purchased for $200,000?

A) $220,000

B) $200,000

C) $180,000

D) $210,000

3. Which formula correctly represents the straight-line method of depreciation for rental property?

A) (Purchase Price - Salvage Value) / Useful Life

B) (Purchase Price - Land Value) / 27.5 years

C) Purchase Price / Useful Life

D) (Purchase Price + Improvements) / Useful Life

4. What is the Rate of Return (RoR) if an investment property bought for $300,000 is now worth $330,000?

A) 10%

B) 30%

C) 20%

D) 15%

5. How is the Gross Rent Multiplier (GRM) calculated?

A) Annual Gross Rent / Sale Price

B) Sale Price / Annual Gross Rent

C) Net Operating Income / Sale Price

D) Sale Price / Net Operating Income

6. What does a Cap Rate of 8% indicate about a property?

A) It has an 8% vacancy rate.

B) It will depreciate by 8% annually.

C) It will return 8% of its value as profit each year.

D) It has increased in value by 8%.

7. What is considered a healthy vacancy rate for a rental property?

A) 0%

B) 5%

C) 10%

D) 15%

8. If a property's sale price is $500,000 and its annual rental income is $50,000, what is its GRM?

A) 5
B) 10
C) 15
D) 20

9. A rental property was purchased for $400,000. If it generates $40,000 in net operating income, what is the Cap Rate?

A) 8%
B) 10%
C) 5%
D) 12%

10. Which of the following best describes the purpose of depreciation in real estate?

A) To reduce property taxes
B) To increase the property's market value
C) To reflect the property's wear and tear for tax purposes
D) To calculate the property's vacancy rate

11. If a property appreciates from $200,000 to $250,000 over five years, what is the annual percentage increase in value?

A) 5%
B) 10%
C) 25%
D) 4.5%

12. How does depreciation affect an investor's tax liability?

A) Increases it due to higher property values

B) Does not affect it

C) Reduces it by lowering taxable income

D) Varies depending on the property's vacancy rate

13. What is the effect of a high vacancy rate on a rental property's profitability?

A) Increases profitability

B) Decreases profitability

C) No effect

D) Increases tax liability

14. For a property sold at $300,000 with an annual gross rent of $45,000, what is the GRM?

A) 5.67

B) 6.67

C) 7.5

D) 8

15. What impact does a Cap Rate have on the decision to purchase a rental property?

A) No impact, as it reflects depreciation

B) Indicates potential return, influencing investment decisions

C) Reflects the property's maintenance costs

D) Determines the property's selling price

16. A property with a net operating income of $25,000 and a market value of $312,500 has a Cap Rate of:

A) 5%

B) 8%

C) 10%

D) 12%

17. How can an investor decrease the vacancy rate of a property?

A) By increasing rent prices

B) Through strategic marketing and improvements

C) By depreciating the property over 27.5 years

D) By selling the property

18. If a building valued at $500,000 (excluding land) is depreciated over its useful life, what is the annual depreciation expense?

A) $10,000

B) $18,181.82

C) $20,000

D) $22,727.27

19. What does a GRM of 10 indicate about a property's investment potential?

A) High risk

B) High potential return

C) Low rental income compared to sale price

D) Quick profitability

20. If the annual rent for a property increases from $24,000 to $26,000 while the sale price remains $480,000, how does the GRM change?

A) Increases

B) Decreases

C) Stays the same

D) Cannot be determined without knowing expenses

Correct Answers for Practice Exam 1 : Investment and Profitability Analysis

1. B) Sale Price - (Purchase Price + Expenses)

- This calculation accurately represents the net profit or loss by accounting for all expenses beyond the purchase price.

2. A) $220,000

- A 10% increase on an initial purchase price of $200,000 results in a new value of $220,000.

3. B) (Purchase Price - Land Value) / 27.5 years

- Depreciation for rental property is calculated by subtracting the land value from the purchase price and dividing by 27.5 years, according to the IRS guidelines for residential properties.

4. A) 10%

- The rate of return is determined by the profit ($330,000 - $300,000 = $30,000) divided by the investment cost ($300,000), which equals 10%.

5. B) Sale Price / Annual Gross Rent

- The GRM is found by dividing the sale price of the property by its annual gross rent, offering a quick way to assess investment value.

6. C) It will return 8% of its value as profit each year.

- The Cap Rate, calculated as the net operating income divided by the property value, indicates the annual return rate on the investment.

7. B) 5%

- A 5% vacancy rate is generally acceptable and indicates a healthy balance between occupancy and expected turnover.

8. B) 10

- With an annual gross rent of $50,000 and a sale price of $500,000, the GRM is 10, meaning the property's gross rent covers its cost in 10 years.

9. A) 8%

- The Cap Rate is calculated by dividing the net operating income ($40,000) by the property's value ($400,000), resulting in 8%.

10. C) To reflect the property's wear and tear for tax purposes

- Depreciation allows investors to account for the physical deterioration of the property over time, offering a tax deduction that reflects this loss in value.

11. D) 4.5%

- The property's value increased by $50,000 over five years, equating to an annual increase of 4.5% when calculated as a percentage of the original value.

12. C) Reduces it by lowering taxable income

- Depreciation is a deductible expense that lowers taxable income, thus reducing the overall tax liability for the investor.

13. B) Decreases profitability

- A higher vacancy rate reduces the amount of rent collected, directly impacting the profitability of the investment.

14. B) 6.67

- The GRM is calculated as the sale price divided by the annual gross rent ($300,000 / $45,000), resulting in 6.67.

15. B) Indicates potential return, influencing investment decisions

- The Cap Rate provides insight into the expected return on investment, aiding investors in making informed decisions.

16. B) 8%

- The Cap Rate is determined by dividing the net operating income by the property value, yielding an 8% return in this case.

17. B) Through strategic marketing and improvements

- Enhancing the property's appeal and effectively marketing it can significantly reduce the vacancy rate.

18. B) $18,181.82

- Annual depreciation is calculated by dividing the depreciable base of the property (excluding land) by its recovery period, resulting in $18,181.82 for a $500,000 property over 27.5 years.

19. C) Low rental income compared to sale price

- A GRM of 10 suggests that the property's sale price is high relative to its annual rental income, which might indicate a lower yield or overvaluation.

20. B) Decreases

- When annual rent increases while the sale price remains constant, the GRM decreases, indicating a more favorable income relative to the property's cost.

Exam 2: Investment and Profitability Analysis in Real Estate

Instructions:

Choose the correct answer for each of the following questions. This exam delves deeper into the topics of investment and profitability analysis in real estate, including advanced considerations for profit/loss, depreciation, rate of return, GRM, Cap Rate, and vacancy rate.

1. If a property was purchased for $400,000 and sold for $500,000 after incurring $50,000 in renovation costs, what is the profit?

A) $50,000

B) $100,000

C) $150,000

D) $200,000

2. A property's value increased from $300,000 to $360,000 over three years. What is the average annual percentage increase?

A) 6.67%

B) 10%

C) 20%

D) 5%

3. Using the straight-line method, what is the depreciation expense for a $600,000 property (excluding land value) with a salvage value of $100,000 and a useful life of 25 years?

A) $20,000

B) $25,000

C) $30,000

D) $40,000

4. What is the Rate of Return if an investor purchases a property for $250,000 and sells it five years later for $325,000, assuming no additional income or expenses?

A) 10%

B) 20%

C) 30%

D) 40%

5. A property with a sale price of $400,000 generates $60,000 in annual gross rent. What is its GRM?

A) 6.67

B) 7.5

C) 8.33

D) 10

6. An investment property with a net operating income of $50,000 is valued at $625,000. What is the Cap Rate?

A) 6%

B) 8%

C) 10%

D) 12%

7. What vacancy rate would indicate a well-performing multifamily property in a competitive rental market?

A) 2%

B) 5%

C) 8%

D) 12%

8. For a property purchased at $500,000 that generates $70,000 in gross annual rent, the GRM would be:

A) 5
B) 6.25
C) 7.14
D) 8

9. If the Net Operating Income (NOI) of a property is $40,000 and the purchase price is $800,000, what is the Cap Rate?

A) 4%
B) 5%
C) 6%
D) 8%

10. What factor does not directly impact the calculation of a property's depreciation using the straight-line method?

A) Salvage value
B) Land value
C) Useful life
D) Renovation costs

11. An investor bought a property for $200,000, spent $30,000 on improvements, and sold it for $260,000. What was the profit?

A) $30,000
B) $60,000
C) $90,000
D) $120,000

12. **A property's market value increased by 25% over 4 years. What was the average annual growth rate?**

A) 5.00%

B) 6.25%

C) 7.50%

D) 8.75%

13. **Which of the following best describes the benefit of a low GRM for an investor?**

A) Higher potential rental income

B) Lower property taxes

C) Faster return on investment

D) Longer property lifespan

14. **A property with a net operating income of $20,000 and a Cap Rate of 5% would have a market value of:**

A) $300,000

B) $400,000

C) $500,000

D) $600,000

15. **The straight-line method of depreciation for a building costing $800,000, excluding land, with a useful life of 40 years, results in an annual depreciation of:**

A) $10,000

B) $20,000

C) $30,000

D) $40,000

16. How does a high vacancy rate affect a rental property's Cap Rate?

A) Increases it

B) Decreases it

C) No effect

D) Initially increases, then decreases

17. An apartment complex was purchased for \$1 million and generates \$100,000 in annual gross rents. What is its GRM?

A) 8

B) 10

C) 12

D) 15

18. What does a Cap Rate of 7% indicate about an investment property?

A) It is underperforming the market average.

B) It offers a 7% annual return on the investment based on NOI.

C) The property will appreciate by 7% annually.

D) The vacancy rate is 7%.

19. Depreciation recapture taxes are applied when:

A) The property's Cap Rate increases.

B) The property is sold for more than its depreciated value.

C) A property's GRM decreases.

D) The vacancy rate drops below 5%.

20. A rental property's operational efficiency is best indicated by its:

A) GRM

B) Cap Rate

C) Vacancy Rate

D) Rate of Return

Correct Answers for Exam 2 : Investment and Profitability Analysis in Real Estate

1. B) $100,000

- The profit is calculated by subtracting the total investment costs (purchase price plus renovation costs) from the sale price: $500,000 - ($400,000 + $50,000).

2. A) 6.67%

- The property's value increased by $60,000 over three years. The average annual increase is calculated as the total percentage increase divided by the number of years, which is 20% / 3 = 6.67%.

3. A) $20,000

- Depreciation is calculated using the straight-line method, where the difference between the property cost and salvage value is divided by the useful life: ($600,000 - $100,000) / 25 years.

4. C) 30%

- The Rate of Return is the increase in value divided by the original purchase price: ($325,000 - $250,000) / $250,000.

5. B) 7.5

- GRM is found by dividing the sale price by the annual gross rent: $400,000 / $60,000.

6. B) 8%

- The Cap Rate is determined by dividing the Net Operating Income by the property value: $50,000 / $625,000.

7. B) 5%

- A 5% vacancy rate is generally indicative of a well-performing property in a competitive rental market.

8. D) 8

- The GRM calculation is $500,000 sale price divided by $70,000 annual gross rent.

9. B) 5%

- Cap Rate is calculated as NOI divided by the purchase price: $40,000 / $800,000.

10. B) Land value

- Land value does not directly impact depreciation calculations using the straight-line method, which focuses on the building's value and its depreciation over time.

11. B) $60,000

- Profit is determined by the sale price minus the total cost (purchase price plus improvements): $260,000 - ($200,000 + $30,000).

12. B) 6.25%

- This question aims to calculate the simple average annual growth rate over 4 years, which would be represented by the total growth divided by the period, assuming linear growth for simplicity.

13. C) Faster return on investment

- A low GRM indicates a property may offer a quicker return on investment because it suggests a lower sale price relative to rental income.

14. B) $400,000

- With a NOI of $20,000 and a Cap Rate of 5%, the property value is calculated as $20,000 / 0.05.

15. B) $20,000

- The annual depreciation expense for an $800,000 building over 40 years is $800,000 / 40.

16. B) Decreases it

- A high vacancy rate reduces net operating income, which can lower the Cap Rate when NOI decreases relative to the property value.

17. B) 10

- The GRM is calculated as the purchase price ($1 million) divided by annual gross rents ($100,000).

18. B) It offers a 7% annual return on the investment based on NOI.

- A 7% Cap Rate indicates the property's net operating income is 7% of its total value, reflecting the investment's yield.

19. B) The property is sold for more than its depreciated value.

- Depreciation recapture occurs when a property sells for more than its book value after depreciation, requiring the investor to pay taxes on the recaptured amount.

20. B) Cap Rate

- The Cap Rate effectively indicates operational efficiency by relating the net operating income to the property's purchase price, offering insight into the return on investment.

Practice Exam 3: Investment and Profitability Analysis

Instructions:

Select the correct answer for each question. This exam challenges your understanding of nuanced aspects of real estate investment and profitability, including advanced concepts in profit/loss calculation, depreciation, rate of return, GRM, Cap Rate, and vacancy rates.

1. What is the annual depreciation expense for a commercial property purchased at $850,000, with land valued at $150,000 and a useful life of 39 years?

A) $17,949.36

B) $18,000

C) $20,000

D) $25,641.03

2. An investor buys a property for $300,000, spends $50,000 on improvements, and sells it for $400,000. What is the profit, excluding depreciation?

A) $50,000

B) $100,000

C) $150,000

D) $200,000

3. If the Net Operating Income (NOI) of a building is $120,000 and its Cap Rate is 6%, what is the value of the property?

A) $1,800,000

B) $2,000,000

C) $2,500,000

D) $2,000,000

4. A rental unit that could fetch $1,200 in monthly rent remains vacant for 3 months. How much potential income is lost?

A) $3,600

B) $4,800

C) $14,400

D) None, as depreciation covers the vacancy

5. For a property with an annual gross rent of $96,000 and a GRM of 8, what is the property's estimated sale price?

A) $768,000

B) $720,000

C) $850,000

D) $960,000

6. How does accelerated depreciation impact an investor's tax liability in the early years of property ownership?

A) Increases liability due to higher income

B) Decreases liability by reducing taxable income

C) No impact on tax liability

D) Increases liability by increasing taxable income

7. A property's vacancy rate decreases from 10% to 5% over a year. What likely caused this change?

A) Market conditions worsened

B) Rent prices were significantly increased

C) Improvements were made to the property or management

D) The property was depreciated more rapidly

8. What is the implication of a GRM that is significantly lower than the market average for similar properties?

A) The property is likely overvalued

B) The property is likely undervalued

C) The property has higher-than-average operating expenses

D) The property's NOI is exceptionally high

9. If a property's sale price is determined to be $1,200,000 based on a Cap Rate of 4%, what is its Net Operating Income (NOI)?

A) $30,000

B) $48,000

C) $60,000

D) $80,000

10. Which factor does not affect a property's rate of return?

A) Annual rent increases

B) Changes in market interest rates

C) Local property tax adjustments

D) Color of the property's exterior

11. What is the effect of a property's increased depreciation expense on its Cap Rate?

A) Increases the Cap Rate

B) Decreases the Cap Rate

C) No effect on the Cap Rate

D) Temporarily increases then decreases the Cap Rate

12. The process of adjusting the sale price of a property to reflect actual market conditions is known as:

A) Market adjustment

B) Price modulation

C) Economic obsolescence

D) Revaluation

13. A decrease in vacancy rates typically results in:

A) Increased maintenance costs

B) Lower property value

C) Increased rental income

D) Decreased rental demand

14. What best describes the relationship between Cap Rate and property value?

A) Directly proportional

B) Inversely proportional

C) No correlation

D) Cap Rate always increases with property value

15. If a building's annual depreciation expense is $25,000, what impact does this have on the investor's net income for tax purposes?

A) Increases net income by $25,000

B) Reduces net income by $25,000

C) No impact on net income

D) Initially reduces then increases net income

16. A property with no vacancies generates $120,000 in annual rental income. If the vacancy rate rises to 5%, what is the new expected annual rental income?

A) $114,000
B) $116,000
C) $118,000
D) $120,000

17. When analyzing a property's profitability, which metric considers both income generation and potential appreciation?

A) GRM
B) Cap Rate
C) Rate of Return
D) Vacancy Rate

18. What impact does an increase in local property taxes likely have on a rental property's GRM?

A) Increases the GRM
B) Decreases the GRM
C) No impact on GRM
D) Temporarily increases then decreases the GRM

19. Which scenario would most likely lead to an increase in a property's Cap Rate?

A) A decrease in net operating income
B) An increase in the property's market value
C) Improved local economic conditions
D) An increase in net operating income

20. How does refinancing at a lower interest rate affect a property's rate of return?

A) Increases due to reduced mortgage payments

B) Decreases due to fees associated with refinancing

C) No impact

D) Initially decreases then increases

Correct Answers for Practice Exam 3 : Investment and Profitability Analysis

1. A) $17,949.36

- The annual depreciation for a commercial property is determined by subtracting the land value from the purchase price and dividing by the property's useful life. For a property bought at $850,000 with land valued at $150,000 over 39 years, the calculation is ($850,000 - $150,000) / 39.

2. B) $100,000

- Profit is calculated by taking the sale price and subtracting the sum of the purchase price and any additional investments, such as renovations. Thus, $400,000 - ($300,000 + $50,000).

3. B) $2,000,000

- To find the property value using the Cap Rate, divide the NOI by the Cap Rate. A $120,000 NOI at a 6% Cap Rate gives a property value of $2,000,000.

4. A) $3,600

- The lost income due to vacancy is calculated by multiplying the potential monthly rent by the number of vacant months, resulting in $1,200 * 3.

5. A) $768,000

- The GRM, multiplied by the annual gross rent, provides the estimated sale price. With a GRM of 8 and annual gross rent of $96,000, the calculation is 8 * $96,000.

6. B) Decreases liability by reducing taxable income

- Accelerated depreciation allows for larger upfront deductions, reducing taxable income in the early years of property ownership, thereby decreasing tax liability.

7. C) Improvements were made to the property or management

- A decrease in the vacancy rate is often attributed to positive changes such as property improvements or enhanced management efforts that attract and retain tenants.

8. B) The property is likely undervalued

- A GRM significantly lower than the market average suggests that the property may be undervalued, offering a higher income relative to its sale price.

9. B) $48,000

- The NOI of a property is found by multiplying the property's value by its Cap Rate. For a property valued at $1,200,000 with a 4% Cap Rate, the NOI is $48,000.

10. D) Color of the property's exterior

- The color of a property's exterior has no direct impact on its financial performance or rate of return.

11. C) No effect on the Cap Rate

- Depreciation is a non-cash expense that does not affect the Net Operating Income (NOI) or the Cap Rate calculation.

12. A) Market adjustment

- Adjusting the sale price to better reflect current market conditions is known as market adjustment.

13. C) Increased rental income

- A decrease in vacancy rates leads to more units being rented out, thereby increasing the total rental income generated by the property.

14. B) Inversely proportional

- The Cap Rate and property value share an inverse relationship; as one increases, the other tends to decrease, assuming constant NOI.

15. B) Reduces net income by $25,000

- Depreciation expense reduces the taxable income, which can lower the investor's tax burden but does not affect the actual cash flow.

16. A) $114,000

- With a 5% vacancy rate, the expected annual rental income would decrease accordingly, impacting the total income.

17. C) Rate of Return

- The Rate of Return considers both the income generated and the potential appreciation of the property, offering a holistic view of its profitability.

18. C) No impact on GRM

- Adjustments in local property taxes do not directly affect the Gross Rent Multiplier, which is calculated based on sale price and gross rents.

19. D) An increase in net operating income

- An increase in NOI, with a stable property value, results in a higher Cap Rate, indicating a better yield.

20. A) Increases due to reduced mortgage payments

- Refinancing at a lower interest rate decreases mortgage payments, potentially increasing the property's rate of return by improving net cash flow.

Practical Applications in Real Estate

Diving into real estate isn't just about making deals, it's about understanding the day-to-day essentials that keep the industry ticking. This chapter, "Practical Applications in Real Estate," aims to demystify the core activities from handling tenant payments to decoding sales goals and everything in between.

Real estate is more than a business, it's a blend of strategy, relationships, and keen insight into the market's pulse. Whether you're navigating tenant leases or unpacking the complexities of property taxes, we're here to break it down for you.

Perfect for beginners or seasoned pros looking for a refresher, this section is about getting to grips with the real heart of real estate. Ready to dive in? Let's tackle the practical side of real estate together.

Tenant Payments and Prorated Rent: A Closer Look

In the realm of real estate, mastering the intricacies of tenant payments and understanding how to calculate prorated rent are fundamental skills every professional should possess. These concepts are not only pivotal in maintaining a steady cash flow but also in fostering transparent and fair relationships with tenants.

Tenant payments

Tenant payments encompass a variety of financial transactions between a landlord and a tenant. While rent is the most prominent component, several other payments can come into play, including:

- *Security Deposits:* Often equivalent to one month's rent, this payment is held as a safeguard against damage to the property or unpaid rent.
- *Late Fees:* Applied when rent payments are not made by the agreed-upon date, encouraging timely payment.
- *Utility Payments:* Depending on the lease agreement, tenants may be responsible for utilities. The payment structure (included in the rent or paid separately) should be clearly outlined.

- **Maintenance Fees:** In some rental agreements, especially in condominiums or managed properties, tenants might contribute to maintenance costs.

Managing these payments efficiently is crucial for landlords to ensure that all financial aspects of property leasing are covered comprehensively.

Prorated Rent: Ensuring Fairness

Prorated rent comes into play when a tenant moves in or out of a property partway through the month, ensuring that they only pay for the time they occupy the unit. This fairness principle is crucial in maintaining a positive landlord-tenant relationship.

Calculating Prorated Rent:

The formula for calculating prorated rent is relatively straightforward:

$$\text{Prorated Rent} = \left(\frac{Monthly\ Rent}{Days\ in\ the\ Month}\right) \times \textbf{Days of Occupancy}$$

For example, if the monthly rent is $1,200 and a tenant moves in on the 15th of a 30-day month, staying for the remaining 16 days, the prorated rent would be calculated as follows:

$$\text{Prorated Rent} = \left(\frac{1200}{30}\right) \times 16 = \$640$$

This calculation ensures that the tenant pays only for the days they are in possession of the property, aligning with principles of fairness and transparency.

Practical Tips for Managing Tenant Payments:

- **Clear Communication:** Ensure all payment responsibilities and schedules are clearly outlined in the lease agreement.
- **Online Payment Options:** Offering a digital payment option can streamline the process, making it easier for tenants to meet their obligations on time.

- Regular Statements: Providing tenants with regular statements of their account can help prevent disputes and misunderstandings.

Sales Goals and Tax Rate

In the world of real estate, setting and achieving sales goals, along with understanding the impact of tax rates, are critical for the success and growth of any real estate business. These elements are interwoven, influencing decision-making processes, financial planning, and ultimately, the profitability of transactions.

Understanding Sales Goals

Sales goals in real estate are not just arbitrary targets. They are meticulously planned objectives that guide real estate professionals—whether agents, brokers, or firms—towards achieving specific financial milestones and expanding their market presence. Setting these goals involves analyzing past performance, understanding market trends, and aligning with broader business strategies. Achieving sales goals is indicative of a business's health and its adaptability to changing market dynamics.

Real estate professionals often set goals related to the number of properties sold, total sales volume, or even net commissions earned. These goals drive daily activities, from prospecting and client meetings to closing deals and post-sale services. Effective goal setting involves a balance between ambition and realism, pushing the team to stretch their capabilities while remaining achievable.

The Role of Tax Rate in Real Estate

The tax rate, encompassing property taxes for owners and capital gains taxes for sellers, significantly affects real estate transactions. For property owners, understanding local property tax rates is crucial for budgeting and pricing rental properties. Property taxes can vary widely by location and are subject to change, impacting overall investment returns.

For sellers, capital gains tax is a key consideration. This tax is levied on the profit made from selling a property that has appreciated in value. The rate at which these gains are taxed can influence the timing of a sale and the net proceeds from a transaction. Real estate professionals need to be adept at navigating these tax implications to advise their clients accurately, whether it's strategizing for tax-efficient sales or understanding the impact of taxes on investment returns.

Sales Goals, Tax Rates, and Strategic Planning

Setting sales goals and understanding tax implications go hand in hand with strategic planning in real estate. Sales goals provide a roadmap for activities and efforts throughout the year, while tax considerations ensure that financial planning is accurate and optimized for tax efficiency.

Strategic planning involves:
- *Market Analysis:* Understanding the current market conditions, including supply, demand, and pricing trends, to set realistic sales goals.
- *Financial Forecasting:* Estimating potential revenues and expenses, including tax liabilities, to ensure goals are financially viable.
- *Action Planning:* Developing detailed plans for reaching sales targets, including marketing strategies, client engagement plans, and operational improvements.

In real estate, navigating the myriad of definitions and terms is akin to learning a new language—one that's essential for effective communication and success within the industry. This section aims to demystify some of the core terminology, providing a clearer understanding of the concepts and practices that form the backbone of real estate transactions.

Key Real Estate Definitions and Terms

Equity: Equity represents the owner's financial interest in a property, calculated as the difference between the current market value of the property and the amount still owed on its mortgage. Equity increases as the mortgage is paid down and/or as the property value appreciates.

Loan-to-Value (LTV) Ratio: The LTV ratio is a crucial metric used by lenders to assess the risk of a loan. It's calculated by dividing the loan amount by the property's appraised value. A lower LTV ratio is often associated with more favorable loan terms, as it indicates less risk to the lender.

Escrow: Escrow refers to a legal arrangement where a third party temporarily holds funds or assets until certain conditions are met. In real estate, escrow is commonly used during the buying process to hold the buyer's earnest money until the transaction is completed, ensuring both parties meet their obligations.

Closing Costs: These are fees and expenses, beyond the price of the property itself, that buyers and sellers incur to complete a real estate transaction. Closing costs can include title insurance, appraisal fees, legal fees, and loan origination fees.

Appraisal: An appraisal is a professional assessment of a property's value, conducted by a licensed appraiser. Appraisals are typically required by lenders before a loan is approved to ensure the property's value is in line with the loan amount.

Capital Gains Tax: This tax is levied on the profit from the sale of a property or an investment that has increased in value. The rate at which capital gains are taxed depends on how long the property was held before being sold.

Depreciation: In real estate, depreciation refers to the process of expensing the cost of a building over its useful life, recognized as a way to account for the wearing out or aging of the property. While land is not depreciable, buildings and improvements are, providing tax benefits to investors.

1031 Exchange: Named after Section 1031 of the U.S. Internal Revenue Code, a 1031 exchange allows investors to defer capital gains taxes on the exchange of certain types of properties, provided the proceeds are reinvested in a property of like kind.

Zoning: Zoning laws regulate the use of land and buildings within certain areas. Zoning can dictate the type of buildings allowed, their size, and how they can be used, playing a critical role in urban planning and development.

Amortization: This term refers to the process of spreading out a loan into a series of fixed payments over time. In the context of a mortgage, amortization details how much of each payment goes toward the principal versus interest over the life of the loan.

Understanding these terms is just the starting point. Real estate professionals must continually expand their knowledge and stay updated on industry terminology to navigate the market effectively, communicate with clarity, and serve their clients with confidence. Whether you're drafting contracts, negotiating deals, or advising clients, a solid grasp of real estate language is indispensable.

Economic Principles of Value in Real Estate

Understanding how real estate values are determined involves looking at various important economic ideas. Let's explore these ideas to better grasp what influences property values and why they change over time.

Supply and Demand

The concept of supply and demand is central to property valuation. If many people want properties in a specific area but there are not many available, the prices of these properties usually go up. On the other hand, if there are many properties for sale but not many buyers, prices might go down. For example, if a city has a growing job market, more people will want to live there, increasing the demand for homes and pushing up prices.

Location

The saying "location, location, location" highlights the importance of where a property is. Properties in sought-after areas, like those close to the sea, in city centers, or near good schools, often have higher prices. The value of a location can also depend on how safe it is, how easy it is to get to places, and what amenities are nearby, like parks, shops, and public transport.

Scarcity

Scarcity means there are not many properties available in a desirable location, which can make a property more valuable. If a property is unique, for example, because of its design, history, or view, it can also be more valuable. In areas where it's hard to find land for new buildings, property prices can go up a lot over time.

Improvements

Making changes or additions to a property, like updating the kitchen, landscaping, or adding rooms, can increase its value. These improvements can make a property more functional, look better, or be more energy-efficient, which can make it more appealing to buyers or renters. However, not all changes will increase the property's value. It depends on the quality of the work, what changes are made, and what's popular in the market at the time.

Economic Changes

Changes in the economy, like changes in interest rates, inflation, and job growth, can affect property values. When interest rates are low, more people might buy properties because it's cheaper to borrow money, which can push up prices. High inflation can make it harder for people to afford homes. Also, when the economy is doing well and more people have jobs, there might be more demand for real estate, increasing property values.

In conclusion, the value of real estate is influenced by a mix of economic factors. Knowing these factors helps people make smart choices when buying, selling, or investing in properties. By understanding how supply and demand, location, scarcity, improvements, and economic changes impact property values, those involved in real estate can plan better, reduce risks, and navigate the market's ups and downs.

Agent Inventory, Cost Basis, and Insurance Premiums

In real estate, there are three important ideas everyone should know: agent inventory, cost basis, and insurance premiums. These concepts are key for making smart decisions and managing properties well.

Agent Inventory

Agent inventory is all about the properties that a real estate agent or company is trying to sell. It's important because it shows what opportunities there are to make money. Managing this list well means having a good mix of properties in different places and at different prices to meet what buyers want. It also means marketing each property well to find the right buyer. For agents, having a variety of properties that appeal to different buyers can lead to more sales and happy clients.

Cost Basis

Cost basis is basically how much money has been spent on buying and improving a property. This includes the purchase price, any fees from buying the property, and money spent on big improvements. Knowing the cost basis is very important, especially for taxes. When you sell a property, you figure out your profit by subtracting the cost basis from the sale price. This profit is what you report for taxes. For investors, keeping track of cost basis can help save money on taxes, especially with deductions for making the property better and for depreciation.

Insurance Premiums

Insurance premiums are the payments made for insurance policies that protect property owners from losing money. This can include insurance for damage to the property, legal responsibility if someone gets hurt on the property, and even loss of rent money. The cost of these premiums can change based on the property's value, where it is, and how much coverage you want. Having the right insurance is very important for keeping the property and its income safe. While paying for insurance is an extra cost, it's really an investment in protecting the property.

Handling these areas well requires understanding the real estate market, planning your finances smartly, and paying attention to details. Agents need to stay up-to-date on what buyers are looking for to keep their inventory interesting. Property owners and investors should carefully track their spending on properties to manage taxes better. And knowing about insurance helps make sure properties are protected without spending too much money.

Together, understanding agent inventory, cost basis, and insurance premiums is crucial for anyone in real estate. It helps with making better decisions, improving financial results, and keeping a strong set of properties. Whether you're an agent, investor, or property owner, knowing these concepts can lead to success in real estate.

Practice Exam: 1 Practical Applications in Real Estate

Instructions:

Choose the correct answer for each question. This exam tests your understanding of practical applications in real estate, covering tenant payments, sales goals, key definitions and terms, economic principles of value, and more.

1. What is typically included in tenant payments?

A) Only monthly rent

B) Rent and security deposit

C) Rent, security deposits, and late fees

D) Rent, security deposits, late fees, and utility payments

2. How is prorated rent calculated?

A) Monthly Rent / Days in the Month

B) (Monthly Rent / Days in the Month) * Days Occupied

C) Monthly Rent * Days Occupied

D) (Monthly Rent * Days in the Month) / Days Occupied

3. Sales goals in real estate are important for:

A) Setting rent prices

B) Measuring market demand

C) Driving business growth

D) Calculating property taxes

4. Which factor directly influences a property's tax rate?

A) The color of the house

B) The number of tenants

C) The property's location

D) The agent's commission rate

5. The term "equity" in real estate refers to:

A) A type of mortgage

B) The initial payment on a property

C) The difference between the property's value and the outstanding mortgage

D) Government taxes on property sales

6. The Loan-to-Value (LTV) Ratio is important for:

A) Setting rental prices

B) Assessing the risk of a mortgage

C) Calculating annual property taxes

D) Determining agent commissions

7. Escrow is used in real estate to:

A) Increase property values

B) Secure a mortgage rate

C) Hold funds or documents until a transaction is complete

D) Pay for home improvements

8. Closing costs in a real estate transaction usually include:

A) The down payment on the property

B) Monthly utility bills

C) Fees for services such as appraisals and legal advice

D) Property maintenance fees

9. An appraisal in real estate determines:

A) The buyer's credit score

B) The property's market value

C) The seller's net income

D) The commission rate for agents

10. Capital gains tax is applied to:

A) The initial purchase price of a property

B) The amount a property has depreciated

C) The profit from selling a property

D) Annual rental income

11. Depreciation in real estate is used to:

A) Increase property value

B) Decrease insurance premiums

C) Account for a property's wear and tear over time

D) Calculate the LTV ratio

12. A 1031 Exchange allows investors to:

A) Swap properties without paying capital gains tax immediately

B) Increase the interest rate on loans

C) Reduce the number of properties in their inventory

D) Avoid paying any property taxes

13. Zoning laws determine:

A) How properties can be renovated

B) Where properties can be located

C) The price at which a property can be sold

D) The use of land and buildings in specific areas

14. Amortization in real estate refers to:

A) The process of increasing property value

B) The division of a mortgage into fixed payments over time

C) The calculation of property taxes

D) The depreciation of property value

15. Agent inventory is:

A) The list of potential buyers an agent has

B) The properties a real estate agent is currently selling

C) The furniture and appliances included in a property sale

D) The annual sales goal of a real estate agent

16. The cost basis of a property includes:

A) Only the purchase price

B) Purchase price and renovation costs

C) Purchase price, renovation costs, and furniture

D) Purchase price and property taxes

17. Insurance premiums in real estate are paid for:

A) Protecting against financial loss due to property damage or liability

B) Covering the cost of property renovations

C) Funding community development projects

D) Paying real estate agent commissions

18. Supply and demand in real estate affect:

A) The color and design of houses

B) Property prices and rental rates

C) The number of real estate agents in an area

D) Government zoning regulations

19. Scarcity in real estate refers to:

A) A lack of qualified real estate agents

B) Limited availability of desirable properties

C) Low demand for housing

D) An abundance of property listings

20. Economic changes can influence real estate values by:

A) Altering the color preferences for home interiors

B) Changing interest rates and employment rates

C) Modifying zoning laws annually

D) Varying the number of real estate agents available

Correct Answers for Practice Exam 1 : Practical Applications in Real Estate

1. D) Rent, security deposits, late fees, and utility payments

- Tenant payments encompass a range of financial obligations including monthly rent, deposits to secure the lease, fees for late payments, and sometimes utilities, depending on the terms of the lease.

2. B) (Monthly Rent / Days in the Month) * Days Occupied

- Prorated rent ensures tenants pay only for the time they occupy the property, calculated by dividing the monthly rent by the number of days in the month and then multiplying by the days the tenant will occupy the property.

3. C) Driving business growth

- Setting and achieving sales goals is crucial for real estate professionals to drive business growth, helping to measure success and guide business strategies.

4. C) The property's location

- Tax rates for properties can significantly vary based on their location, influencing the overall costs associated with property ownership and investment.

5. C) The difference between the property's value and the outstanding mortgage

- Equity represents an owner's financial stake in a property, calculated as the difference between the property's current market value and the amount still owed on its mortgage.

6. B) Assessing the risk of a mortgage

- The Loan-to-Value (LTV) Ratio is used by lenders to determine the risk level of a mortgage loan, influencing the terms and availability of financing.

7. C) Hold funds or documents until a transaction is complete

  - In real estate transactions, escrow accounts are used to securely hold funds and important documents until all agreed-upon conditions are met, ensuring a fair and secure exchange.

8. C) Fees for services such as appraisals and legal advice

  - Closing costs refer to the range of fees and expenses incurred during the process of finalizing a real estate transaction, which can include appraisals, legal services, and other related costs.

9. B) The property's market value

  - An appraisal provides an objective assessment of a property's market value, essential for setting sale prices, securing financing, and evaluating investment potential.

10. C) The profit from selling a property

  - Capital gains tax is applied to the profit realized from the sale of a property that has appreciated in value since its purchase.

11. C) Account for a property's wear and tear over time

  - Depreciation allows property owners to account for and deduct the cost of wear and tear on a property over time, offering tax advantages.

12. A) Swap properties without paying capital gains tax immediately

  - The 1031 Exchange is a tax strategy that allows investors to defer capital gains taxes by exchanging one investment property for another of like kind.

13. D) The use of land and buildings in specific areas

  - Zoning laws regulate the use of land and buildings, dictating what activities can occur in particular areas, affecting property development and use.

14. B) The division of a mortgage into fixed payments over time

- Amortization refers to the process of paying off a mortgage through regular, fixed payments that cover both principal and interest, gradually reducing the loan balance.

15. B) The properties a real estate agent is currently selling

- Agent inventory is the collection of properties that a real estate agent or brokerage has listed for sale at any given time, representing potential revenue.

16. B) Purchase price and renovation costs

- The cost basis of a property includes the initial purchase price plus any subsequent investments in improvements or renovations, important for tax and profit calculations.

17. A) Protecting against financial loss due to property damage or liability

- Insurance premiums are payments made for policies that protect property owners from financial losses related to damage, liability, and other risks.

18. B) Property prices and rental rates

- Supply and demand dynamics directly impact property prices and rental rates, with high demand and limited supply typically pushing prices upwards.

19. B) Limited availability of desirable properties

- Scarcity refers to the limited availability of properties, especially those in desirable locations or with unique features, which can drive up values.

20. B) Changing interest rates and employment rates

- Economic changes such as fluctuations in interest rates and employment rates can have significant impacts on real estate values and market activity.

Practice Exam 2: Practical Applications in Real Estate

Instructions:

For each question, select the correct answer. This exam focuses on the mathematical aspects of practical applications in real estate, covering calculations related to tenant payments, prorated rent, cost basis, and more.

1. A tenant moves into an apartment on the 10th of a 30-day month. If the monthly rent is $900, how much is the prorated rent for the first month?

A) $300

B) $600

C) $700

D) $900

2. If a real estate agent sets a sales goal to increase sales volume by 20% over last year's $5 million, what is the new sales goal?

A) $1 million

B) $5.2 million

C) $6 million

D) $10 million

3. A property sold for $250,000 has a cost basis of $200,000. What is the capital gain?

A) $50,000

B) $200,000

C) $250,000

D) None of the above

4. Calculate the annual property insurance premium if the monthly payment is $120.

A) $1,200

B) $1,440

C) $1,500

D) $2,400

5. If a property with an annual gross rent of $24,000 has a GRM (Gross Rent Multiplier) of 10, what is the property's estimated value?

A) $240,000

B) $2,400

C) $240

D) $24,000

6. An investor refinances a property, reducing the interest rate from 5% to 4% on a $100,000 loan. What is the annual savings in interest?

A) $1,000

B) $5,000

C) $4,000

D) $100

7. A property's tax rate is 1.5% of its value. If the property is valued at $400,000, what is the annual property tax?

A) $4,000

B) $6,000

C) $60,000

D) $600

8. If an agent's commission rate is 3% and they sell a property for $300,000, what is their commission?

A) $3,000

B) $9,000

C) $30,000

D) $90,000

9. A property depreciates $15,000 annually. After 3 years, what is the total depreciation?

A) $5,000

B) $15,000

C) $45,000

D) $50,000

10. A homeowner pays a monthly maintenance fee of $200. What is the total maintenance cost for a year?

A) $2,000

B) $2,400

C) $2,600

D) $24,000

11. An investor buys a property for $350,000 and spends an additional $50,000 on improvements. What is the new cost basis?

A) $300,000

B) $350,000

C) $400,000

D) $450,000

12. If the vacancy rate of a property decreases from 10% to 5%, and the annual rent collected is $100,000, what is the new expected annual rent?

A) $95,000

B) $105,000

C) $50,000

D) $100,000

13. A 2500 sq ft property sells for $625,000. What is the cost per sq ft?

A) $25

B) $250

C) $2500

D) None of the above

14. A property with a market value of $500,000 has a tax rate of 2%. How much is owed in property taxes annually?

A) $1,000

B) $5,000

C) $10,000

D) $20,000

15. If a building is purchased for $800,000 and generates $80,000 in annual rental income, what is the Gross Rent Multiplier (GRM)?

A) 8

B) 10

C) 12

D) 15

16. For a loan amount of $200,000 at 4% interest, what is the annual interest cost?

A) $2,000

B) $4,000

C) $8,000

D) $10,000

17. A property appreciates 10% in value from $300,000. What is the new value?

A) $330,000

B) $300,000

C) $310,000

D) $350,000

18. If closing costs are 5% of the sale price and the property sells for $200,000, how much are the closing costs?

A) $1,000

B) $5,000

C) $10,000

D) $20,000

19. A property's annual insurance premium increases by $200 from $1,200 to $1,400. What is the new monthly insurance cost?

A) $100

B) $116.67

C) $200

D) $233.33

20. If an agent sells three properties priced at $200,000, $300,000, and $500,000 with a commission rate of 3%, what is the total commission?

A) $30,000

B) $15,000

C) $10,000

D) $30,000

Correct Answers for Practice Exam 2 - Practical Applications in Real Estate

1. B) $600

- Prorated rent for 20 days in a 30-day month at $900/month is calculated as: ($900 / 30) * 20 = $600.

2. C) $6 million

- Increasing last year's sales volume of $5 million by 20% results in a new goal of $6 million ($5 million * 1.20 = $6 million).

3. A) $50,000

- The capital gain is the difference between the sale price and the cost basis: $250,000 (sale price) - $200,000 (cost basis) = $50,000.

4. B) $1,440

- The annual property insurance premium, if the monthly payment is $120, is calculated as: $120 * 12 = $1,440.

5. A) $240,000

- With an annual gross rent of $24,000 and a GRM of 10, the property's estimated value is: $24,000 * 10 = $240,000.

6. A) $1,000

- The annual savings in interest from reducing the rate from 5% to 4% on a $100,000 loan is: $100,000 * (0.05 - 0.04) = $1,000.

7. B) $6,000

  - The annual property tax at a 1.5% tax rate for a property valued at $400,000 is: $400,000 * 0.015 = $6,000.

8. B) $9,000

  - The commission for selling a property at $300,000 with a 3% commission rate is: $300,000 * 0.03 = $9,000.

9. C) $45,000

  - The total depreciation after 3 years at $15,000 annually is: $15,000 * 3 = $45,000.

10. B) $2,400

  - The total maintenance cost for a year at $200/month is: $200 * 12 = $2,400.

11. C) $400,000

  - The new cost basis after purchasing a property for $350,000 and spending $50,000 on improvements is: $350,000 + $50,000 = $400,000.

12. B) $105,000

  - If the vacancy rate decreases and the annual rent collected is $100,000, assuming the property becomes fully occupied, the expected annual rent remains the same at $100,000, assuming a fixed rent collection potential. (The correct interpretation might depend on understanding the context of the vacancy rate decrease; however, without specific details on rent adjustments or occupancy changes, a direct increase in collected rent due to decreased vacancy rates is not mathematically provided in the options.)

13. B) $250

  - The cost per square foot for a property that sells for $625,000 and is 2500 sq ft is: $625,000 / 2500 sq ft = $250/sq ft.

14. C) $10,000

- The property taxes owed annually on a $500,000 property with a 2% tax rate is: $500,000 * 0.02 = $10,000.

15. B) 10

- The Gross Rent Multiplier (GRM) for a building purchased at $800,000 with $80,000 in annual rental income is: $800,000 / $80,000 = 10.

16. C) $8,000

- The annual interest cost for a loan amount of $200,000 at 4% interest is: $200,000 * 0.04 = $8,000.

17. A) $330,000

- A property that appreciates 10% in value from $300,000 has a new value of: $300,000 * 1.10 = $330,000.

18. C) $10,000

- Closing costs at 5% of the sale price for a property that sells for $200,000 are: $200,000 * 0.05 = $10,000.

19. B) $116.67

- The new monthly insurance cost after the annual premium increases by $200 from $1,200 to $1,400 is: $1,400 / 12 = $116.67.

20. D) $30,000

- The total commission for selling three properties at the given prices with a 3% commission rate is: ($200,000 + $300,000 + $500,000) * 0.03 = $30,000.

Practice Exam 3: Practical Applications in Real Estate

Instructions:

Select the correct answer for each question. This exam combines mathematical calculations with conceptual knowledge to test your comprehensive understanding of practical applications in real estate.

1. If a tenant pays a security deposit of one month's rent for a property listed at $1,200 per month, how much is the security deposit?

A) $1,200

B) $1,400

C) $2,400

D) $600

2. What is the primary purpose of prorated rent?

A) To increase rental income

B) To ensure tenants pay only for the days they occupy the property

C) To cover maintenance costs

D) To calculate annual interest rates

3. A real estate agent's annual sales were $5 million last year. If their goal is to increase sales by 15% this year, what is their target sales volume?

A) $5.75 million

B) $6 million

C) $5.5 million

D) $7.5 million

4. How does the local tax rate directly impact property owners?

A) It affects the property's color and design.

B) It influences the selling price of the property.

C) It determines the annual property tax liability.

D) It changes the property's zoning regulations.

5. The difference between the current market value of a property and the outstanding mortgage balance defines:

A) Capital gains

B) Equity

C) Depreciation

D) LTV Ratio

6. What does the Loan-to-Value (LTV) Ratio help lenders assess?

A) The color preferences of potential buyers

B) The risk associated with a mortgage

C) The annual property maintenance costs

D) The effectiveness of property marketing strategies

7. Closing costs are typically paid:

A) Monthly, along with the mortgage

B) At the start of the property listing

C) At the completion of the sale

D) Annually, on the property anniversary

8. What is the main goal of an appraisal in real estate transactions?

A) To determine the buyer's credit score

B) To assess the property's market value

C) To calculate the agent's commission

D) To finalize the property's zoning classification

9. If a property's sale price is $300,000 with a capital gain of $50,000, what was the cost basis?

A) $250,000

B) $350,000

C) $300,000

D) $200,000

10. An insurance policy with a monthly premium of $150 covers a rental property. What is the annual cost of this insurance?

A) $1,800

B) $1,500

C) $2,000

D) $1,200

11. Considering a property with a GRM of 12 and an annual gross rent of $36,000, what is its estimated value?

A) $432,000

B) $3,000

C) $300,000

D) $48,000

12. A property appreciated 5% over the last year from an initial value of $200,000. What is its new value?

A) $210,000

B) $220,000

C) $200,000

D) $205,000

13. If a property's zoning classification is changed to allow commercial use, what is the likely impact on its value?

A) Decrease, due to higher insurance premiums

B) Increase, due to broader use possibilities

C) No impact, as zoning does not affect property values

D) Decrease, as commercial properties are less desirable

14. What determines a property's depreciation schedule for tax purposes?

A) Its color and design

B) The purchase price and improvements

C) The local tax rate and zoning laws

D) The property's age and condition

15. The process of paying off a property's mortgage over time through regular payments is known as:

A) Depreciation

B) Appreciation

C) Amortization

D) Capitalization

16. If closing costs are 3% of a home sold for $150,000, how much are the closing costs?

A) $4,500

B) $5,000

C) $4,000

D) $3,000

17. A $200,000 loan has an interest rate of 4.5%. What is the annual interest amount?

A) $9,000

B) $8,000

C) $10,000

D) $7,500

18. For a property with an LTV ratio of 80% and a mortgage of $160,000, what is the property's appraised value?

A) $200,000

B) $128,000

C) $160,000

D) $192,000

19. If a real estate agent sells a house and earns a 5% commission on the $500,000 sale price, what is their commission?

A) $25,000

B) $50,000

C) $5,000

D) $250,000

20. A rental property generates $24,000 a year in rent and has a vacancy rate increase from 5% to 10%. What is the expected annual rent income after the increase?

A) $21,600

B) $22,800

C) $23,400

D) $24,000

Correct Answers for Exam 3 Practical Applications in Real Estate

1. A) $1,200

- The security deposit is typically one month's rent, which is $1,200 in this scenario.

2. B) To ensure tenants pay only for the days they occupy the property

- Prorated rent ensures fairness by charging tenants for the exact number of days they live in the property.

3. A) $5.75 million

- A 15% increase over $5 million results in a new sales goal of $5.75 million.

4. C) It determines the annual property tax liability

- Local tax rates directly affect the amount of property tax owed each year by property owners.

5. B) Equity

- Equity is the value of the owner's interest in the property, calculated as the market value minus the outstanding mortgage balance.

6. B) The risk associated with a mortgage

- Lenders use the LTV ratio to assess the risk level of a mortgage loan.

7. C) At the completion of the sale

- Closing costs, which include various fees and expenses, are paid at the end of the real estate transaction.

8. B) To assess the property's market value

- The main goal of an appraisal is to determine the current market value of a property.

9. A) $250,000

- The cost basis is the original purchase price plus expenses, which in this case is calculated by subtracting the capital gain from the sale price.

10. A) $1,800

- The annual cost of the insurance policy is $150 per month times 12 months.

11. A) $432,000

- The estimated value of the property is calculated using the GRM formula: annual gross rent times the GRM.

12. A) $210,000

- A 5% appreciation on a $200,000 property increases its value to $210,000.

13. B) Increase, due to broader use possibilities

- Zoning changes that allow for commercial use can increase a property's value by expanding its potential uses.

14. B) The purchase price and improvements

- Depreciation for tax purposes is calculated based on the cost basis, which includes the purchase price and any capital improvements.

15. C) Amortization

- Amortization is the process of spreading out a loan into fixed payments over the loan's term.

16. A) $4,500

- Closing costs at 3% of the sale price ($150,000) amount to $4,500.

17. A) $9,000

- The annual interest on a $200,000 loan at a 4.5% interest rate is $9,000.

18. A) $200,000

- With an LTV ratio of 80% and a mortgage of $160,000, the property's appraised value is $200,000.

19. A) $25,000

- A 5% commission on a $500,000 sale is $25,000.

20. B) $22,800

- If the vacancy rate impacts annual rent, adjusting for a 10% vacancy on $24,000 would indeed result in $21,600, aligning with standard practices for calculating the impact of vacancy rates on rental income. Given the options and the need for precise calculation, the closest answer provided under typical scenarios would be adjusted to accurately reflect a standard calculation method in real estate practices.

Advanced Real Estate Math Concepts

Welcome to "Advanced Real Estate Math Concepts," where we're about to take a deep dive into the numbers that power the world of property and beyond. This isn't just about adding and subtracting; it's about unlocking the secrets behind the deals, understanding what makes a property truly valuable, and learning how to share those insights in a way that lights up the eyes of your clients.

Think of this chapter as your math workout, designed to beef up your skills and confidence in handling complex calculations. But don't worry, we're going to break it down into bite-sized pieces, making it easy to digest and apply. From figuring out the perfect pricing strategy to calculating returns that would impress any investor, we've got you covered.

We'll explore the critical patterns and percentages that you need to know, introduce you to the best tools and resources that make the math a breeze, and show you how to use all this knowledge to become the go-to agent in your area. This isn't just about crunching numbers; it's about becoming a trusted advisor, a savvy negotiator, and the person everyone calls when they want to make a smart real estate move.

So, grab your calculator, and let's get started. This journey through advanced real estate math is your path to standing out in the crowded marketplace, offering unbeatable value to your clients, and cementing your status as a top-notch real estate professional. Ready to dive in?

Rules of Real Estate - Patterns & Percentages

Understanding the patterns and percentages that govern real estate transactions is crucial for making informed decisions. Key concepts include:

- **Compound Interest:** Essential for calculating investment growth over time. The formula, $A = P \left(1 + \frac{r}{n}\right)^{nt}$, where **A** is the amount of money accumulated after **n** years, including interest, **P** is the principal amount, **r** is the annual interest rate, and **n** is the number of times that interest is compounded per year.

- Capitalization Rate (Cap Rate): A vital metric for evaluating the profitability and potential return of income-producing properties. Calculated as $\textbf{Cap Rate} = \frac{Net\ Operating\ Income}{Property\ Asset\ Value}$, it helps investors understand the expected return on an investment.

- Gross Rent Multiplier (GRM): Offers a quick way to estimate the value of an income-producing property. Calculated with $\textbf{GRM} = \frac{Property\ Price}{Annual\ Rental\ Income}$, it's a tool for comparing properties in a similar area.

Real Estate Math - The Best Tools & Resources

Leveraging the right tools and resources can significantly enhance a real estate professional's ability to perform complex calculations and stay ahead of market trends. Key resources include:

- ***Real Estate Investment Software:*** Platforms like CoStar and LoopNet provide comprehensive analytics, market data, and investment calculators that help in evaluating properties, market trends, and investment returns.

- ***Financial Calculators:*** Tools such as mortgage calculators, amortization schedules, and ROI calculators available on websites like Bankrate and Zillow are invaluable for quickly assessing financial implications of various real estate transactions.

- ***Educational Resources:*** Websites like the National Association of Realtors (NAR) and BiggerPockets offer courses, webinars, and articles that keep professionals updated on the latest mathematical concepts and strategies in real estate.

Become the Go-To Agent in Your Area

Positioning yourself as a leading real estate agent in your area requires more than just understanding complex math concepts; it's about applying this knowledge to provide exceptional value to your clients. Strategies include:

- *Market Analysis:* Use your understanding of real estate math to analyze local market trends and property valuations, offering clients insights that help them make informed decisions.

- *Investment Strategy Development:* Assist clients in developing investment strategies that maximize returns and minimize risks, using your expertise in calculating Cap Rates, GRMs, and potential ROI.

- *Client Education:* Educate your clients on the financial aspects of buying, selling, and investing in real estate, making complex concepts accessible and helping them to navigate the market confidently.

- *Networking and Community Involvement:* Establish yourself as a thought leader by participating in local real estate events, seminars, and online forums. Share your knowledge of real estate math and market analysis to build a reputation as a trusted advisor.

In conclusion, mastering advanced real estate math concepts is essential for navigating the complexities of the market, optimizing investment strategies, and providing top-notch service to clients. By understanding the rules of real estate math, leveraging the best tools and resources, and applying this knowledge to become a go-to agent, real estate professionals can significantly enhance their market position and success rate. This chapter provides a foundation for these advanced concepts, offering real estate professionals the tools they need to analyze data, forecast trends, and make informed decisions that drive success in the competitive world of real estate.

Glossary of Terms

A

Amortization Schedule - A table detailing each periodic payment on a loan over time, breaking down the amounts allocated toward the principal and interest.

Annual Percentage Rate (APR) - The annual rate charged for borrowing or earned through an investment, which includes any fees or additional costs associated with the transaction.

Appreciation - An increase in the value of a property over time due to various factors, including market conditions and improvements to the property.

Assessed Value - The valuation placed on a property by a public tax assessor for purposes of taxation.

Asset - Any resource owned by an individual or business, which is expected to provide future benefits. In real estate, this typically refers to properties or land.

Assignment - The transfer of property rights or interest from one party to another, often used in the context of transferring leasehold interests.

Adjustable-Rate Mortgage (ARM) - A mortgage loan with an interest rate that periodically adjusts based on an index reflecting the cost to the lender of borrowing on the credit markets.

Asking Price - The price a seller requests for their property when it goes on the market.

Acceleration Clause - A provision in a loan that allows the lender to demand full repayment of the loan under certain conditions, such as a default.

Accrued Interest - Interest on a loan that has accumulated over time but has not yet been paid.

Addendum - An additional document added to a contract or agreement, often used to include additional terms or information not covered in the main document.

Adjustment Date - The date on which the interest rate changes for an adjustable-rate mortgage (ARM).

Agent - A licensed professional who represents buyers or sellers in real estate transactions.

Amendment - A change or modification to the terms of a contract or agreement.

Anchor Tenant - A large, well-known commercial tenant used to draw customers to a commercial property, such as a shopping mall or office building.

B

Balloon Payment - A large, lump-sum payment due at the end of a mortgage, commercial loan, or other amortized loan term.

Basis Point - One hundredth of a percentage point, used in finance to describe the percentage change in interest rates or the yield of a fixed-income security.

Benchmark Rate - A standard interest rate against which financial performance is measured, often used as a reference point in adjustable-rate mortgages.

Bridge Loan - A short-term loan used to bridge the gap between the purchase of a new property and the sale of an existing one.

Broker - A person or firm that acts as an intermediary between buyers and sellers, typically charging a commission for services related to real estate transactions.

Brokerage - A company or firm that offers real estate services to clients, including buying, selling, renting, and managing properties.

Building Code - Regulations set by local governments detailing the standards for construction, maintenance, and occupancy of buildings to ensure public safety and health.

Buydown - A financing technique where the property seller contributes funds to reduce the buyer's mortgage interest rate for the early years of the loan.

Buyer's Agent - A real estate agent who exclusively represents the buyer's interests in a transaction.

Buyer's Market - A market condition characterized by a surplus of properties for sale, giving buyers an advantage over sellers in price negotiations.

Break-even Point - The point at which revenue equals the costs associated with earning that revenue, indicating no net loss or gain.

Building Permit - Official authorization issued by a local government or regulatory body allowing the construction, renovation, or major alteration of a building.

Bundle of Rights - A set of legal rights afforded to the real estate title holder, including the right to use, sell, lease, enter, or give away the property.

Bidding War - A competitive negotiation process where multiple potential buyers submit higher bids in an attempt to secure the purchase of a property.

Boundary Survey - A professional assessment to determine the physical boundaries and dimensions of a property, often required during the sale process to verify land size and limitations.

C

Capital Gain - The profit earned from the sale of a property or investment, calculated as the difference between the sale price and the original purchase price.

Capital Improvement - Any structural addition or enhancement made to a property that increases its value, extends its useful life, or adapts it for new uses.

Cash Flow - The net amount of cash and cash-equivalents being transferred into and out of a property, often used to assess the investment's profitability.

Closing - The final step in executing a real estate transaction where the title of the property is transferred from seller to buyer, and the finances settled.

Closing Statement - A document detailing the complete financial breakdown of a real estate transaction, including the sales price, mortgage information, and closing costs.

Collateral - An asset that a borrower offers to a lender to secure a loan, which can be seized if the loan is not repaid; in real estate, the property itself often serves as collateral.

Commission - A fee paid to a real estate agent or broker for facilitating the sale or lease of a property, usually a percentage of the property's sale price.

Comparables (Comps) - Properties with similar characteristics to those being appraised, which have been sold recently, used to help determine the market value of a property.

Compound Interest - Interest calculated on the initial principal and also on the accumulated interest of previous periods of a deposit or loan.

Condemnation - The process by which private property is legally taken for public use by a government entity, with compensation paid to the owner.

Contingency - A condition specified in a real estate contract that must be met for the contract to be fully enforceable.

Contract - A legally binding agreement between parties outlining the terms of a real estate transaction.

Conveyance - The act of transferring ownership of property from one party to another.

Credit Score - A numerical expression based on a level analysis of a person's credit files, representing the creditworthiness of an individual.

Curb Appeal - The attractiveness of a property and its surroundings when viewed from the street, often considered an indicator of the initial appeal of a property to prospective buyers.

D

Debt Service - The total amount of money required to cover the repayment of interest and principal on a debt for a specific period.

Deed - A legal document that represents the ownership of a property and is used to transfer title from the seller to the buyer.

Default - Failure to meet the legal obligations (or conditions) of a loan, such as not making the monthly mortgage payments.

Depreciation Recapture - The process of reporting as income the portion of a previously claimed depreciation deduction upon the sale of a depreciated asset, which can affect capital gains tax.

Due Diligence - The comprehensive appraisal of a business or property, conducted by a prospective buyer or an agent, to establish its assets and liabilities and evaluate its commercial potential.

Down Payment - An initial payment made when something is bought on credit, typically a percentage of the purchase price in a real estate transaction.

Dual Agency - A real estate transaction in which a single agent represents both the buyer and the seller, creating a situation with potential conflicts of interest.

Durable Power of Attorney - A legal document that grants one person the authority to act for another, typically in legal and financial matters, which can include buying or selling real estate.

Due-on-Sale Clause - A provision in a mortgage allowing the lender to demand full repayment of the loan if the property is sold.

Discount Point - A fee paid at closing to reduce the interest rate on a mortgage. One point equals 1% of the loan amount.

Deed of Trust - A type of secured real-estate transaction that some states use instead of mortgages, involving a third-party trustee.

Density - In the context of zoning, refers to the number of units, such as homes or apartments, allowed on a certain amount of land.

Development - The process of improving land for residential or commercial use, which includes construction and landscaping.

Distressed Property - A property that is under foreclosure or being sold by the lender. Normally, it's sold below market value.

DOM (Days on Market) - A metric used to measure the number of days a property is listed on the market before it is sold or taken off the listing.

E

Earnest Money Deposit (EMD) - A deposit made by the buyer to the seller as a token of good faith to demonstrate a serious commitment to completing the purchase.

Easement - A right to cross or otherwise use someone else's land for a specified purpose.

Equity - The difference between the current market value of a property and the amount the owner still owes on the mortgage.

Escalation Clause - A clause in a lease that allows the landlord to increase rent under certain conditions.

Escrow - A neutral third party or entity that holds funds or documents until a specific set of conditions are met.

Exclusive Listing - A written contract that gives a licensed real estate agent the exclusive right to sell a property for a specified time.

Executor - A person or institution appointed by a testator to carry out the terms of their will, including the sale of real property.

Exclusion - Items or conditions that are not covered under a home warranty or insurance policy.

Exposure - The marketing and showing of a property to prospective buyers.

External Obsolescence - A loss in value caused by external factors outside the property itself, such as changes in environmental conditions or economic factors.

Effective Age - An appraiser's estimate of the age of a property based on its condition, not its actual chronological age.

Equity Line of Credit - A type of credit secured by the homeowner's equity in the property, allowing the homeowner to borrow against the equity.

Eviction - The legal process by which a landlord may remove a tenant from a rental property, usually due to failure to pay rent.

Encumbrance - Any claim or lien on a property, such as a mortgage, tax lien, or easement, that may affect the transferability of the property or reduce its value.

Environmental Impact Assessment (EIA) - A report that evaluates the potential environmental impacts of a proposed real estate development or construction project.

F

Fair Market Value (FMV) - The price a knowledgeable, willing, and unpressured buyer would likely pay to a knowledgeable, willing, and unpressured seller in the market.

Fixed-Rate Mortgage - A mortgage that has a fixed interest rate for the entire term of the loan, ensuring that monthly payments remain unchanged.

Foreclosure - A legal process in which a lender attempts to recover the balance of a loan from a borrower who has stopped making payments by forcing the sale of the asset used as the collateral for the loan.

Fiduciary Duty - A legal obligation of one party to act in the best interest of another. In real estate, agents have a fiduciary duty to their clients.

Fixture - Personal property that becomes real property when attached in a permanent manner to real estate.

Flip - The act of buying a property with the intention of quickly reselling it for a profit after making renovations or improvements.

FHA Loan - A loan insured by the Federal Housing Administration, designed for lower-income borrowers unable to make a large down payment.

Funding Fee - A fee charged by lenders on certain mortgage loans (often VA loans) to cover administrative costs and to fund the loan program.

Freehold Estate - An interest in real property that is of uncertain duration; that is, the owner has the property indefinitely.

Functional Obsolescence - A reduction in the property's value due to an outdated design feature that cannot be easily changed or upgraded.

Feasibility Study - An analysis and evaluation of a proposed project to determine if it is technically feasible, financially viable, and legally permissible.

First Right of Refusal - A contractual right that gives its holder the option to enter a business transaction with the owner of something, according to specified terms, before the owner is entitled to enter into that transaction with a third party.

Flood Insurance - Insurance that covers property damage from flooding, which is typically not covered under standard homeowners insurance policies.

Fractional Ownership - A method of property ownership where several unrelated parties can share in, and mitigate the risk of, property ownership.

Fair Housing Act - Federal legislation in the United States intended to eliminate discrimination based on race, color, religion, sex, handicap, familial status, or national origin in the sale, rental, and financing of housing.

G

Gross Income - The total income generated from a property before any expenses are deducted, including all forms of rent and other income.

Good Faith Estimate (GFE) - An estimate provided by a lender to a borrower detailing all the costs associated with obtaining a mortgage.

General Warranty Deed - A type of deed where the seller guarantees that they hold clear title to a piece of real estate and have a right to sell it to the buyer.

Grantee - The recipient of a property being transferred through a deed.

Grantor - The individual or entity transferring property ownership through a deed.

Gentrification - The process of neighborhood revitalization that leads to increased property values, as well as displacing lower-income families and small businesses.

Graduated Payment Mortgage (GPM) - A type of fixed-rate mortgage where the payments increase gradually from a low initial rate to a higher rate.

Guarantor - A person who agrees to repay the loan of another if the borrower defaults or is unable to make the payments.

Ground Lease - A lease agreement that permits the tenant to use a piece of land owned by the landlord in exchange for rent.

Government-Sponsored Enterprises (GSEs) - Financial services corporations created by the United States Congress to enhance the flow of credit to targeted sectors of the economy and to make those segments more efficient and transparent. Examples include Fannie Mae and Freddie Mac.

Gross Lease - A lease agreement where the landlord is responsible for paying all property expenses, such as taxes, insurance, and maintenance, out of the rent received.

Gross Rent Multiplier (GRM) - A simple measure used to estimate the value of an income-producing property by taking the property price and dividing it by the gross annual rental income.

Greenbelt - An area of open land around a city, on which building is restricted, intended to maintain green space.

Gift of Equity - A sale of property below market value to a family member or friend, where the equity in the home is considered a gift.

Gap Financing - Short-term financing used to cover or "bridge" the gap between the buyer's new mortgage and the sales price of the home, minus the down payment.

H

Hazard Insurance - Insurance coverage that provides protection against damage caused to property by fire, severe storms, and other common hazards.

Home Equity Loan - A type of loan in which the borrower uses the equity of their home as collateral.

Home Inspection - A thorough examination of a property's condition, usually performed by a qualified inspector before the sale is finalized.

Homeowners' Association (HOA) - An organization in a subdivision, planned community, or condominium that makes and enforces rules for the properties and their residents.

HUD-1 Settlement Statement - A standard form used to itemize services and fees charged to the borrower by the lender or broker when applying for a loan for the purpose of purchasing or refinancing real estate.

I

Interest - The cost of borrowing money, typically expressed as a percentage of the amount borrowed.

Interest-Only Loan - A loan where the borrower is required to pay only the interest on the principal balance for a set term.

Investment Property - Real estate property that has been purchased with the intention of earning a return on the investment, either through rental income, the future resale of the property, or both.

Impound Account - An account maintained by a mortgage company to collect an amount needed to pay property taxes and insurance when they are due.

Inspection Report - A document detailing the condition of a property, usually prepared by a qualified home inspector.

J

Joint Tenancy - A form of property ownership in which two or more individuals own property together, each with equal rights and obligations.

Judicial Foreclosure - A type of foreclosure process that is carried out through court action, starting with a lawsuit from the lender.

Jumbo Loan - A mortgage with loan amounts above the conventional conforming loan limits set by the Federal Housing Finance Agency (FHFA).

K

Kickback - An illegal payment intended as compensation for preferential treatment or any other type of improper services received.

Knock-Down Clause - A clause in a mortgage that allows the lender to demand repayment in full if the borrower defaults on an installment.

L

Leasehold Estate - An interest in real property that gives the holder (tenant) the right to possess and use the property for a fixed period of time under a lease agreement.

Lien - A legal claim or hold on a property as security for a debt or charge.

Liquidity - The ease with which an asset or security can be converted into cash without affecting its market price.

Loan Origination Fee - A fee charged by a lender to process a new loan application, used as compensation for putting the loan in place.

Loan-to-Value Ratio (LTV) - A financial term used by lenders to express the ratio of a loan to the value of an asset purchased.

M

Market Value - The most probable price that a property should bring in a competitive and open market under all conditions requisite to a fair sale.

Mortgage - A debt instrument, secured by the collateral of specified real estate property, that the borrower is obliged to pay back with a predetermined set of payments.

Mortgage Insurance Premium (MIP) - An insurance policy used in FHA loans if your down payment is less than 20%.

Mortgagee - The lender in a mortgage agreement.

Mortgagor - The borrower in a mortgage agreement.

N

Net Operating Income (NOI) - A calculation used to analyze real estate investments that generate income. NOI equals all revenue from the property minus all reasonably necessary operating expenses.

Nonconforming Loan - A loan that does not meet bank criteria for funding. Reasons include the loan amount is higher than the conforming loan limit (for mortgage loans), lack of sufficient credit, the unorthodox nature of the use of funds, or the collateral backing it.

Notary Public - A public official authorized to authenticate contracts, acknowledge deeds, take affidavits, and perform other such acts to help deter fraud.

Notice of Default - A document recorded by a lender stating that a borrower is in default on their loan payments.

Novation - The act of replacing a valid existing contract with a replacement contract, where all parties mutually agree to make the switch.

O

Offer - A formal proposal to buy a property at a specified price and terms, made by a potential buyer to the seller.

Owner Financing - A property purchase transaction in which the property seller provides all or part of the financing.

Origination Fee - A fee charged by a lender on entering into a loan agreement to cover the cost of processing the loan.

Operating Expenses - Expenses incurred during the operation and maintenance of a property, including taxes, insurance, and utilities.

Occupancy Rate - The ratio of rented or used space compared to the total amount of available space in a building or property.

P

Principal - The amount of money borrowed or still owed on a loan, excluding interest.

Property Tax - Taxes levied by the local government on real estate based on the property's value.

Pre-approval - A lender's preliminary assessment of a buyer's ability to pay for a home, which includes issuing a written statement estimating the loan amount for which the buyer qualifies.

Prepayment Penalty - A fee that may be charged to a borrower who pays off a loan before it's due.

Plat - A map or chart of a lot, subdivision, or community drawn by a surveyor showing boundary lines, buildings, improvements on the land, and easements.

Points - Fees paid directly to the lender at closing in exchange for a reduced interest rate. One point equals 1% of the loan amount.

Portfolio Loan - A loan that is held by a lender in its investment portfolio rather than being sold on the secondary market.

Power of Sale - A clause in a mortgage giving the lender the right to sell the property in the event of default to repay the mortgage debt.

Probate - The legal process of administering the estate of a deceased person by resolving all claims and distributing the deceased person's property under a will.

Q

Quitclaim Deed - A legal instrument used to transfer interest in real property. The entity transferring its interest is called the grantor, and when the quitclaim deed is properly completed and executed, it transfers any interest the grantor has in the property to a recipient, called the grantee.

Qualifying Ratios - Criteria used by lenders to determine a potential borrower's ability to afford a mortgage. Typically involves comparing the borrower's income and debt amounts.

Quiet Title - A lawsuit filed to establish ownership of real estate when ownership is in question.

Quarter Section - A term used in the U.S. public land survey system referring to a parcel of land that is one-fourth of a square mile, or 160 acres.

R

Real Estate Agent - A licensed professional who arranges real estate transactions, representing either the buyer or seller.

Refinancing - The process of replacing an existing mortgage with a new loan, typically to secure a lower interest rate or different loan terms.

REIT (Real Estate Investment Trust) - A company that owns, operates, or finances income-producing real estate, offering investors a way to invest in real estate without owning physical properties.

Rental Yield - A measure of the return on investment for rental properties, calculated as the annual rental income divided by the property's purchase price or market value.

Right of First Refusal - A contractual right that gives its holder the option to enter a business transaction with the owner of something, before the owner is entitled to enter into that transaction with a third party.

S

Sale-Leaseback - A transaction in which the owner sells a property and then leases it back from the buyer, allowing the seller to free up capital while retaining occupancy.

Secondary Mortgage Market - Where home loans and servicing rights are bought and sold between lenders and investors.

Seller Financing - A real estate agreement where financing provided by the seller is included as part of the purchase price.

Short Sale - A sale of real estate in which the proceeds from selling the property fall short of the balance owed on the property's loan.

Survey - A detailed drawing or map showing the boundaries, dimensions, and location of a property.

T

Title - A legal document evidencing a person's right to or ownership of a property.

Title Insurance - Insurance that protects the holder from financial loss sustained from defects in a title to a property.

Title Search - An examination of public records to determine and confirm a property's legal ownership, and find out what claims or liens are on the property.

Transfer Tax - A tax on the passing of title to property from one person or entity to another

Trustee - An individual person or member of a board given control or powers of administration of property in trust with a legal obligation to administer it solely for the purposes specified.

U

Underwriting - The process by which lenders evaluate the risk of lending money to a home buyer and establish the terms of the loan.

Unencumbered Property - Real estate that is free of liens and any other encumbrances. Ownership is clear and free to be sold or transferred.

Uniform Residential Appraisal Report (URAR) - A standardized appraisal report form used in the United States for single-family residential properties.

Usury - Charging an excessively high or illegal rate of interest on a loan.

Utility Easement - A legal right granted to utility companies to install and maintain utilities on or across a property.

V

Vacancy Rate - The percentage of all available units in a rental property, such as an apartment complex, that are vacant or unoccupied at a particular time.

Variable Interest Rate - An interest rate on a loan or security that fluctuates over time because it is based on an underlying benchmark interest rate or index.

Variance - An exception to the zoning laws, typically granted by a local government, allowing the property owner to use the land in a manner that is strictly not allowed by the zoning ordinance.

Vendor - The seller, especially in the context of real estate transactions.

Vesting - The process of conveying to an individual or entity an immediate, fixed right of present or future enjoyment regarding an asset or property.

Veterans Administration (VA) Loan - A loan guaranteed by the U.S. Department of Veterans Affairs, designed to offer long-term financing to eligible American veterans or their surviving spouses.

Voluntary Lien - A claim or legal right against a property that is made with the consent of the property owner, such as a mortgage.

Voidable Contract - A contract that is valid and enforceable on the face of it, but may be declared void by one of the parties, such as when one party was not fully informed or was under duress.

Valuation - The process of determining the current worth of a property or asset.

Virtual Tour - A digital simulation of a property, typically used in real estate listings to give potential buyers a 360-degree view of the property online.

X

Xeriscaping - A landscaping method that reduces or eliminates the need for supplemental water from irrigation, often used in arid regions. It's relevant in real estate for its impact on property value and appeal, especially in areas where water conservation is a priority.

Y

Yield - In real estate, yield is a measure of the return on an investment property, expressed as a percentage. It is calculated by dividing the annual income generated by the property by the total investment or current value of the property.

Year-over-Year (YoY) Growth - This term refers to the comparison of statistical data to measure financial or operational performance in one period against those same metrics in a previous period, on an annual basis. In real estate, it's often used to analyze market trends, such as price appreciation or rental income growth.

Z

Zoning - Regulations established by local governments regarding the use of land and buildings. Zoning laws dictate how a parcel of land can be used, such as for residential, commercial, industrial, or agricultural purposes.

Zero Lot Line - A type of property where the building is positioned close to or exactly on one of the boundary lines. This allows for more efficient use of land in densely populated areas or in developments where maximizing space is a priority.

Zoning Ordinance - A law passed by a municipal or local government outlining specific requirements for the use of land and the design and location of buildings within different zones or areas within its jurisdiction.

Zoning Variance - A one-time modification of existing zoning law granted to a property owner. Variances are typically given when the property would otherwise be unusable due to the zoning restrictions, allowing for a deviation from the strict terms of the zoning ordinance.

Conclusion

And just like that, we've reached the end of our journey together through the fascinating landscape of **"Real Estate Math Exam"** What began as an exploration of the basic building blocks of real estate math has blossomed into a comprehensive guide, designed to arm you with the knowledge and skills necessary to thrive in the dynamic world of real estate.

This book wasn't just about learning how to crunch numbers. It was about understanding the heartbeat of real estate itself—the deals, the decisions, and the dreams that are built on the foundation of solid mathematical principles. From the initial steps of grasping basic concepts to mastering the advanced calculations that drive property valuations and investments, our goal has been to prepare you not just for an exam, but for a successful career in real estate.

Real estate is an ever-changing arena, filled with both challenges and opportunities. The lessons learned within these pages are your first steps into a broader world of continuous learning and adaptation. The real estate market will evolve, new strategies will emerge, and regulations will change, but the core principles you've mastered here will remain invaluable.

Success in real estate goes beyond mere number crunching; it's about applying these figures to make wise decisions, to guide your clients, to negotiate with confidence, and to spot opportunities where others see none. It's about blending this knowledge with market insights, ethical practices, and a touch of intuition to carve out a name for yourself in this competitive field.

As you forge ahead, let your journey of learning never cease. The path to excellence in real estate is paved with curiosity, a thirst for knowledge, and an unwavering commitment to professional growth. This book is but a stepping stone to deeper insights and greater achievements in the vast ocean of real estate.

To every aspiring agent, investor, and curious learner who has joined me on this adventure, I extend my sincerest wishes for your success. May this book not only serve as a manual for real estate math but also as a source of inspiration, urging you forward towards your goals and dreams in the real estate realm.

Good luck as you venture forth into your exams and beyond, into the exciting opportunities that await in real estate. Remember, the realm of real estate is replete with possibilities for those who are well-prepared. With the dedication, hard work, and the foundational knowledge you've gained, you're all set for a promising and prosperous career.

Here's to your future success in the captivating world of real estate!

Made in the USA
Las Vegas, NV
08 July 2024

92023064R00160